Windows Powershell for Developers

Douglas Finke

Beijing · Cambridge · Farnham · Köln · Sebastopol · Tokyo

Windows Powershell for Developers
by Douglas Finke

Published by O'Reilly Media, Inc., 1005 Gravenstein Highway North, Sebastopol, CA 95472.

O'Reilly books may be purchased for educational, business, or sales promotional use. Online editions are also available for most titles (*http://my.safaribooksonline.com*). For more information, contact our corporate/institutional sales department: 800-998-9938 or *corporate@oreilly.com*.

Editor: Rachel Roumeliotis	**Cover Designer:** Karen Montgomery
Production Editor: Iris Febres	**Interior Designer:** David Futato
Proofreader: Iris Febres	**Illustrator:** Robert Romano

Revision History for the First Edition:
    2012-07-03   First release
See *http://oreilly.com/catalog/errata.csp?isbn=9781449322700* for release details.

ISBN: 978-1-449-32270-0

[LSI]

1341348370

To my daughter, Elizabeth, with love

Table of Contents

Preface

Windows PowerShell is a successful, compelling, and integrated tool that all good .NET developers, IT pros, and anyone working with Windows should have in their toolboxes.

It can be used for making unit tests more powerful, scripting tasks such as reading XML or data imports, providing integration points in your .NET applications for end users to customize or extend using their own scripts, and defining little languages to express readable and concise business rules.

PowerShell simplifies your life, opening doors not previously accessible to you, by providing a .NET-based scripting language filled with useful features and *application programming interfaces* (APIs) for all the common programming tasks you take on daily.

You'll quickly learn the basic concepts using the interactive command line, and you'll move rapidly to creating scripts and embedding PowerShell into your existing .NET applications.

Audience

This book is for anyone who wants to know more about PowerShell. If you're serious about PowerShell, it's a must read. This book walks you through what is possible with PowerShell—helping you answer questions such as "can this be done better, faster, or simpler, or can I make it repeatable?"—and planting the seeds for you to creatively apply this new distributed automation platform on your own.

Assumptions This Book Makes

This book is not a beginner's guide to PowerShell. If you are an experienced developer or IT pro, this book gives you insight into what PowerShell can do.

The examples in this book are runnable out of the box. You can study how and what the scripts do—this is one of the tried-and-true ways of learning a new paradigm. While some examples include C# .NET, it is not required that you understand C#.

The examples are self-contained. Run them; see what they do. Then you can pull them apart, tweak them, and incorporate them into your PowerShell and .NET solutions.

Contents of This Book

Chapter 1 gives an overview of the platform and answers the question "Why Power-Shell?"

Chapter 2 steps you through getting PowerShell prepped for running.

Chapter 3 offers a walkthrough of things you probably didn't even know the PowerShell platform could do.

Chapter 4 covers writing a template engine and using the new PowerShell v3 abstract syntax tree interface to extract information from PowerShell scripts.

Chapter 5 kicks it up a notch and shows you how easy it is to provide scripting abilities for your C# (WPF) apps by embedding PowerShell into them.

Chapter 6 demonstrates PowerShell's excellent capabilities for working with the Internet. JSON, XML, HTTP, Twitter? No problem.

Chapter 7 demonstrates how PowerShell is based on .NET. Want to build GUIs with less code? This is the chapter for you.

Chapter 8 further explores PowerShell's relationship to .NET and shows you how to leverage this seamless integration with other Microsoft frameworks.

Chapter 9 covers one of my favorite topics—building "little languages"—and shows how PowerShell makes this easy. Whether you prefer domain-specific languages (DSL) or domain-specific vocabularies (DSV), you'll want to check out what PowerShell has to offer.

Chapter 10 shows you how to really leverage applications like Microsoft Excel and by extension, Microsoft COM (Component Object Model) applications.

Chapter 11 is an excursion through some of the new and exciting features of PowerShell v3, set to ship with Windows 8 and Windows Server 2012, and available in beta for Windows 7.

Appendix A is all about programmer productivity. This is a PowerShell sweet spot, and this chapter shows you how to get the most out of the platform.

Appendix B shows you how to enable PowerShell v2 to load and work with .NET 4.0 DLLs. This is the default mode in PowerShell v3.

Conventions Used in This Book

The following typographical conventions are used in this book:

Plain text
> Indicates menu titles, menu options, menu buttons, and keyboard accelerators (such as Alt and Ctrl).

Italic
> Indicates new terms, URLs, email addresses, filenames, file extensions, pathnames, directories, and Unix utilities.

`Constant width`
> Indicates commands, options, switches, variables, attributes, keys, functions, types, classes, namespaces, methods, modules, properties, parameters, values, objects, events, event handlers, XML tags, HTML tags, macros, the contents of files, or the output from commands.

`Constant width bold`
> Shows commands or other text that should be typed literally by the user.

`Constant width italic`
> Shows text that should be replaced with user-supplied values.

 This icon signifies a tip, suggestion, or general note.

 This icon indicates a warning or caution.

Using Code Examples

This book is here to help you get your job done. In general, you may use the code in this book in your programs and documentation. You do not need to contact us for permission unless you're reproducing a significant portion of the code. For example, writing a program that uses several chunks of code from this book does not require permission. Selling or distributing a CD-ROM of examples from O'Reilly books does require permission. Answering a question by citing this book and quoting example code does not require permission. Incorporating a significant amount of example code from this book into your product's documentation does require permission.

We appreciate, but do not require, attribution. An attribution usually includes the title, author, publisher, and ISBN. For example: "*PowerShell for Developers* by Douglas Finke (O'Reilly). Copyright 2012 Douglas Finke, 978-1-4493-2270-0."

If you feel your use of code examples falls outside fair use or the permission given above, feel free to contact us at *permissions@oreilly.com*.

Available for Download

The code examples in the following chapters are available for download from GitHub at *https://github.com/dfinke/powershell-for-developers*.

We'd Like to Hear from You

Please address comments and questions concerning this book to the publisher:

O'Reilly Media, Inc.
1005 Gravenstein Highway North
Sebastopol, CA 95472
(800) 998-9938 (in the United States or Canada)
(707) 829-0515 (international or local)
(707) 829-0104 (fax)

We have a web page for this book, where we list errata, examples, and any additional information. You can access this page at:

http://oreilly.com/catalog/9781449322700

To comment or ask technical questions about this book, send email to:

bookquestions@oreilly.com

For more information about our books, courses, conferences, and news, see our website at *http://www.oreilly.com*.

Find us on Facebook: *http://facebook.com/oreilly*

Follow us on Twitter: *http://twitter.com/oreillymedia*

Watch us on YouTube: *http://www.youtube.com/oreillymedia*

Safari® Books Online

Safari Books Online is an on-demand digital library that lets you easily search over 7,500 technology and creative reference books and videos to find the answers you need quickly.

With a subscription, you can read any page and watch any video from our library online. Read books on your cell phone and mobile devices. Access new titles before they are available for print, and get exclusive access to manuscripts in development and post feedback for the authors. Copy and paste code samples, organize your favorites, download chapters, bookmark key sections, create notes, print out pages, and benefit from tons of other time-saving features.

O'Reilly Media has uploaded this book to the Safari Books Online service. To have full digital access to this book and others on similar topics from O'Reilly and other publishers, sign up for free at *http://my.safaribooksonline.com*.

Acknowledgments

Writing a book is an interesting journey. Now that it's completed, looking back over the last several months I'm amazed at how lucky I've been to come in contact with so many terrific people.

I'd like to thank my editor at O'Reilly, Rachel Roumeliotis, who was absolutely amazing to work with.

Thank you to Elizabeth, my daughter, who has just finished another year at university and continues to be my inspiration.

I was fortunate to have three great guys as reviewers for my book. They spent countless hours providing feedback and examples, researching specific content, offering lots of encouragement, and engaging with me in great discussions about PowerShell.

A special thanks to **Daniel Moore**. His passion for computing has earned him the nickname Beaver (as in "eager beaver"). He jumps in deep-end first and starts building dams like nobody's business. He's responsible for the WPF GUI in Chapter 5, a.k.a. the "Beaver Music application." He helped save me tons of time prepping the code for NuGet and the other examples for GitHub. Thanks, Daniel!

Thank you very much, **Aleksandar Nikolic´** and **Steve Murawski**, fellow PowerShell MVPs and cofounders of *PowerShell Magazine* (*http://www.powershellmagazine.com/*).

Aleksandar's incredible attention to detail was a significant asset in helping to finalize the book. He has a passion for PowerShell and is extremely generous with the time that he spends with the PowerShell community. Catch him at the next PowerShell Deep Dive.

Steve's depth of knowledge on PowerShell let him plow through these chapters and provide great feedback throughout the process.

When Steve signed on to review the book, his family was about to increase by one. He reviewed the chapters, did speaking gigs (including PowerShell Deep Dive), went to his day job, and took care of a newborn. Makes me tired just writing about it.

Gentlemen, it was an honor and privilege working with you.

And Now, the Small Village of Folks Who Helped, Inspired, and Supported Me

Allyson Chisholm—you have my heart.

Sal Mangano—fellow author, how you wrote a 1,000-page book is beyond me.

Thank you to this gang, a group of smart, supportive people whom I continue to learn from: Jeffrey Snover, James Brundage, Bruce Payette, Lee Holmes, Jason Shirk, Ed Wilson, Davin Tanabe, Jason Dolinger, Ravikanth Chaganti, Shay Levy, Ajay Kalras, Joel Bennett, Oisín Grehan, Keith Hill, Karl Prosser, Will Steele, Justin Rich, Lance Arlaus, Peter Coates, Ronald Lindtag, Sivabalan Muthukumar, Bailey Ling, Josh Einstein, and last but not least, Caleb and Ebony Finke (the furry ones).

## CHAPTER 1

Introduction

> *There is nothing more difficult to take in hand, more*
> *perilous to conduct, or more uncertain in its success,*
> *than to take the lead in the introduction of a new order*
> *of things. Because the innovator has for enemies all*
> *those who have done well under the old conditions and*
> *lukewarm defenders in those who may do well under the*
> *new.*
>
> —Nicolo Machiavelli, *The Prince*

PowerShell is the next-generation platform for distributed automation in the Microsoft Windows environment. It provides significant benefits to developers, testers, power users, and administrators. PowerShell works by leveraging the .NET Framework, and provides significant benefits to developers, testers, power users, and administrators. PowerShell leverages .NET to provide a powerful, consistent, intuitive, extensible, and useful set of tools that drive down costs, and make it easier to program for and automate Windows.

PowerShell was developed in 2002 under the code name *Monad*. In 2006, Microsoft published Release Candidate 1 of the platform, simultaneously announcing its new name, Windows PowerShell. Today PowerShell v3 is being delivered with Windows 8 and Windows Server 2012 and is available for Windows 7.

 For a slightly reworked version of inventor Jeffrey Snover's opening to the *Monad Manifesto* whitepaper, which outlined the core ideas behind what would eventually become PowerShell, see *http://bit.ly/n68k1X*.

New PowerShell developers can often create timesaving scripts after just a few hours of learning. There are numerous accounts of people seeing huge reductions in time spent solving problems using PowerShell, compared to traditional system programming languages.

Another distinguishing feature of PowerShell is the fact that you can embed it into .NET applications. Adding the PowerShell scripting engine to a Windows .NET application allows you to provide a full-featured configuration and macro language to that application. This is roughly analogous to adding Visual Basic for Applications (VBA) to automate your work in Microsoft Excel.

This Is Just the Beginning

Once you learn PowerShell, you'll be able to write scripts for any PowerShell-enabled system. Windows Server 2012 is shipping with over 2,300 *cmdlets* (the basic unit of PowerShell functionality), up from the 400 cmdlets that shipped with Windows 2008 R2.

On top of this, the number of PowerShell solutions provided from third parties and the user community is growing by leaps and bounds. To get an idea of what PowerShell's future might hold, check out the sidebar "PowerShell Score Card, Ten Years On" to see what it has accomplished already in its 10-year history.

PowerShell Score Card, Ten Years On

- PowerShell v3 will ship with both Windows 8 and Windows Server 2012. There will be a version available for older Windows platforms.
- PowerShell v1 shipped in 2006.
- PowerShell v2 in 2009.
- WS2012 ships with over 2,300 cmdlets ready to use.
- PowerShell is integrated with SQL Server, IIS, Hyper-V, Microsoft Exchange, SharePoint, Server Manager, and much more.
- PowerShell is a *stop ship event*, meaning no Microsoft server product ships if it does not have a PowerShell interface.
- PowerShell supports running background jobs, running PowerShell scripts remotely, workflows, and much more.
- PowerShell is integrated with third-party companies like VMWare, Intel, Cisco, Citrix, Red Hat, and NetApp, among others.
- PowerShell has third-party tools like IDEs, Quest Software, Devfarm Software, Software/FX, and many more.
- The PowerShell console window runs in the browser, a.k.a. PowerShell Web Access (PWA).
- PowerShell has a thriving community with over 50 PowerShell MVPs (most valuable professionals), bloggers, podcasts, script repositories, active forums, and much more.

Why Use PowerShell

I use PowerShell for a number of reasons. It makes me fast, it's easy to use, and it's comprehensive. While PowerShell will never win a race with compiled .NET code, it's fast enough.

 You can include .NET code directly in a PowerShell script and compile it on the fly.

PowerShell is an astonishing *glue language* because it is rooted in .NET. The .NET Framework, and the applications built on it, provides a set of powerful components that PowerShell can connect together. This includes the .NET applications I am building today. PowerShell pipes objects—not text—across the pipeline, enabling programming scenarios, in few lines of code, that were not possible before.

PowerShell is easy to learn and extremely powerful. It has all the elements you'd expect in a systems language—variables, loops, data structures, file I/O—and more. In addition, it has complete access to the .NET Framework, and the ability to seamlessly load .NET DLLs, instantiate objects, and retrieve metadata—either on your local box or via PowerShell remoting.

Finally, PowerShell is fun, satisfying, and rewarding to use. Whether you're using it to automate a tedious task, to simplify an implementation complicated by traditional means, or to create GUIs (WPF or WinForms based), PowerShell reduces both the effort and time you spend to get to a completed program.

There's a New Game in Town

Think of PowerShell as a new pinball game. We can continue to play the old one—we know how to jiggle the machine just right so as not to tilt it, we understand all the ins and outs, and we know the tricks to get extra plays—but this new game has great potential.

But there is a wrinkle here: in order to get good at PowerShell, you need to experience a short, frustrating period of being bad at it (i.e., the valley of the s-curve shown in Figure 1-1). That means you'll be looking things up, wrapping your head around new ideas, and getting comfortable with the fact that when you jiggle PowerShell, sometimes it's going to tilt.

 Usually you see declines in performance before significant improvements.

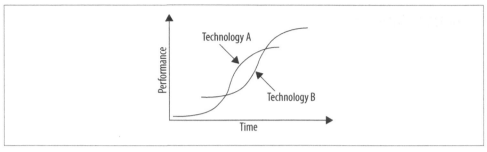

Figure 1-1. S-curve of innovation

An Underutilized Development Tool

Scripted versions of applications require less code, effort, and development time compared to traditional approaches. The interesting discussion is not static languages versus dynamic languages, but rather when and where to use both for delivering solutions. As John Ousterhout, creator of Tcl/Tk, put it:

> Scripting languages are higher level than system programming languages in the sense that a single statement does more work on average. A typical statement in a scripting language executes hundreds or thousands of machine instructions, whereas a typical statement in a system programming language executes about five machine instructions.

In summary, you owe it to yourself to try out this new pinball machine.

## CHAPTER 2

Getting Started

Installing PowerShell

Installing PowerShell is as simple as installing any other application. Even better, it comes preinstalled with Windows 7, Windows Server 2008 R2, Windows 8, and Windows Server 2012. PowerShell is also available for previous versions of Windows XP, 2003, and Vista.

As noted, PowerShell v3 comes preinstalled with Windows 8 (and as I am writing this, there is a RC release for Windows 7; you can download it at *http://bit.ly/MdfXPo*). New cmdlets and language features are abundant in this more robust version, all designed to make you more productive and lower the barrier of entry to using PowerShell.

If you are running an older Microsoft Windows OS, I encourage you to update that; however, PowerShell v2 can run on these boxes. You can get v2 at *http://bit.ly/2QfKYT*; make sure to download the right PowerShell for your OS and architecture.

 While there is no PowerShell version for UNIX, Linux, or Mac, Microsoft did license the PowerShell language under the Community Promise (*http://bit.ly/dLIIIJ8*). We'll see if any developers pick up from here and implement PowerShell on non-Windows boxes.

Checking the PowerShell Version

Depending on your Windows OS, you can navigate to PowerShell in many ways. First, get to the command prompt and type:

```
PS C:\> $PSVersionTable

Name                      Value
----                      -----
WSManStackVersion         3.0
PSCompatibleVersions      {1.0, 2.0, 3.0}
SerializationVersion      1.1.0.1
BuildVersion              6.2.8158.0
```

```
PSVersion                        3.0
CLRVersion                       4.0.30319.239
PSRemotingProtocolVersion        2.103
```

This gives you lots of good information about the PowerShell version running on your box—including what version of .NET you are going against, noted as CLRVersion in PowerShell. I'm running PowerShell v3 CTP3. I can run PowerShell in version 2 mode; if possible, you should too.

Here is what I get when I look at the $PSVersionTable variable. Notice I have only two compatible versions and am using .NET 2.0, CLRVersion. When PowerShell v2 was delivered, only .NET 2.0 was released. PowerShell v3 works with .NET Framework 4.0.

```
PS C:\> $PSVersionTable

Name                             Value
----                             -----
CLRVersion                       2.0.50727.5448
BuildVersion                     6.1.7601.17514
PSVersion                        2.0
WSManStackVersion                2.0
PSCompatibleVersions             {1.0, 2.0}
SerializationVersion             1.1.0.1
PSRemotingProtocolVersion        2.1
```

Interactivity, the Key to PowerShell

The prompt is up, so let's work the PowerShell REPL. A *REPL* (pronounced "repple") is a read-eval-print loop. This means that when you type some PowerShell command and press Enter, those commands are read and evaluated, results (or errors) are printed, and the console loops back and waits to do it again. Let's try it:

```
PS C:\> 2 + 2 * 3
8
PS C:\>
```

So, PowerShell is just a big calculator? Not exactly. If you try that example in a DOS prompt, what happens? You get an error. Here, the result is printed and we get the prompt back, ready to complete your next request.

Now type in the "Hello World" quoted string. Press Enter, and you get back the same thing you typed, without the quotes. PowerShell *evaluated* that for you, demonstrating the *E* in REPL. Also, we didn't have to explicitly specify that we wanted it to be printed; PowerShell just "knew" to do that. These are great timesaving aspects of PowerShell—not to mention, they cut down on keystrokes too.

```
PS C:\> "Hello World"
Hello World
```

Let's tap into the .NET Framework now. Type in:

```
PS C:\> [System.Math]::Pow(2, 3)
8
```

Here, you've input the System.Math namespace and called the static method Pow(). Get used to the syntax; you'll be using it again and again. Square brackets ([]) around the fully qualified type name and two colons (::) indicate that we're calling the static method. This is the syntax the PowerShell team has decided on.

Let's create a variable, set it to a string, and then inspect its type. You may be familiar with the GetType() method from C#.

```
PS C:\> $a = "Hello"
PS C:\> $a.GetType()

IsPublic IsSerial Name    BaseType
-------- -------- ----    --------
True     True     String  System.Object
```

Set the variable $a to the string "Hello"; then, by using the GetType() method, you can verify that $a is a string. This is very handy when running or debugging PowerShell scripts. You can slap a GetType() on a variable and find out exactly what type it is. Now, how to run a PowerShell script?

Running a PowerShell Script

The execution policy is part of PowerShell's security strategy. It determines whether you can load configuration files (including your PowerShell profile) and run scripts, and it determines which scripts, if any, must be digitally signed before they will run.

When you install PowerShell, the execution policy is set by default to Restricted. This means that PowerShell will not load configuration files or run scripts. (If you're new to PowerShell, better safe than sorry.) Even though you are restricted from using scripts, you can still run interactive commands.

Once you are more comfortable with using PowerShell and scripts written by others, you can change the setting.

Changing the Execution Policy from the Command Line

You change the policy by using the Set-ExecutionPolicy cmdlet. You can find more information about the Set-ExecutionPolicy cmdlet by typing the following:

```
Get-Help Set-ExecutionPolicy -Online
```

The cool part is, the -Online parameter will launch the browser and navigate to the cmdlet web page.

RemoteSigned is good for you

There are a few options you can use with the -ExecutionPolicy parameter found on the Set-ExecutionPolicy cmdlet. Many users set the execution policy to RemoteSigned, which means that all scripts and configuration files downloaded from the Internet must be signed by a trusted publisher. This "protects" you so that if you download a script or get one in an email and try to run it, PowerShell will prompt you before letting you continue. As you gain experience, you might choose the Unrestricted setting as follows, but be aware that this comes with risks—you might launch scripts that could disable or destroy information on your system.

```
PS C:\> Set-ExecutionPolicy Unrestricted
```

I run in Unrestricted mode, but I have been working with PowerShell for a few years. I'm comfortable with the scripts I run because I know the authors and trust the sites from which I have downloaded the scripts.

Here's an example of why RemoteSigned is a good idea. Ed Wilson is a Microsoft employee, author of PowerShell books, a blogger for the "Hey, Scripting Guy!" blog (*http://bit.ly/b5qEhd*), and the driving force behind the Windows PowerShell Scripting Games (*http://bit.ly/AoGHwO*). Ed invited me to be a judge at the games. I downloaded one of the entries for review and then ran it. The creator of the script had unintentionally added some WMI code that disabled my Ethernet card. I ran the script and then spent the next hour trying to figure out why I couldn't connect to the Internet and how to re-enable the card.

If had the RemoteSigned execution policy set, PowerShell would have warned me that I was running a script I had downloaded, and I may have chosen not to run it. This is especially handy if you end up with a folder with scripts from mixed sources.

Running scripts with the execution policy set to Restricted

Let's run the test script again with the policy set to Restricted:

```
PS C:\> .\test.ps1
File C:\test.ps1 cannot be loaded because the execution
of scripts is disabled on this system. For more information,
see about_Execution_Policies at
http://go.microsoft.com/fwlink/?LinkID=135170.
At line:1 char:1
+ .\test.ps1
+ ~~~~~~~~~~
    + CategoryInfo          : NotSpecified: (:) [], PSSecurityException
    + FullyQualifiedErrorId : UnauthorizedAccess
```

You can set the execution policy to one of several settings so you don't get this message and can run the script. You'll need to do a little research to figure out which setting is most appropriate for you. You need to *run the console as administrator* in order to effect the Set-ExecutionPolicy changes because it is a Registry setting.

Here are all the possible options for the -ExecutionPolicy parameter on the Set-ExecutionPolicy cmdlet.

Restricted   Does not load configuration files or run scripts. Restricted is the default execution policy.

AllSigned	Requires that all scripts and configuration files be signed by a trusted publisher, including scripts that you write on the local computer.
RemoteSigned	Requires that all scripts and configuration files downloaded from the Internet be signed by a trusted publisher.
Unrestricted	Loads all configuration files and runs all scripts. If you run an unsigned script that was downloaded from the Internet, you are prompted for permission before it runs.
Bypass	Nothing is blocked, and there are no warnings or prompts.
Undefined	Removes the currently assigned execution policy from the current scope. This parameter will not remove an execution policy that is set in a Group Policy scope.

Now we're set to run a script

Let's try a simple script. The script *test.ps1* contains the quoted string "Hello World".

```
PS C:\> Get-Content .\test.ps1
"Hello World"

PS C:\> .\test.ps1
Hello World
```

To run a PowerShell script, you'll need to place ".\" before the name of the script to indicate that it is in the current directory. Alternatively, you can provide the full path to the script. In other words, scripts can be specified by full path or relative path.

Again, notice that there is no compilation step—you just execute and go. Even though there is no compilation step and PowerShell is a dynamic language, it is based on .NET, which proves to be beneficial in many ways.

PowerShell works within the .NET Framework and thus we can perform *reflection* at the command line using Get-Member (see more on this cmdlet in Chapter 3), similar to how we can use the GetType() method to see the underlying .NET object type we're manipulating. Reflection is the process by which you can observe (i.e., do type introspection) and modify an object's structure and behavior at runtime. Here, we just did some observing.

PowerShell ISE

Windows PowerShell *Integrated Scripting Environment* (ISE; pronounced "ice") is free and available as soon as you install PowerShell, or immediately if you are using Microsoft operating systems like Windows 7 or Windows 8 that have PowerShell already installed.

ISE is a graphical host application for PowerShell. It lets you run commands and write, edit, run, test, and debug scripts in an environment that displays syntax in colors and that supports Unicode.

ISE is designed for users at all levels of proficiency. Beginners will appreciate the syntax colors and the context-sensitive Help. Multiline editing makes it easy to try the examples that you copy from the Help topics and from other sources. Advanced users will appreciate the availability of multiple execution environments, the built-in debugger, and the extensibility of the ISE object model.

Other PowerShell Editors

PowerShell does have a few free editors specifically tailored for use with it. There are a number of other editors that support the editing of many different programming languages, and typically the PowerShell community has stepped up to deliver extensions for syntax highlighting, build tools, and more.

PowerGUI (http://powergui.org/index.jspa)
> PowerGUI is an extensible graphical administrative console for managing systems based on PowerShell. These systems include Windows OS (XP, 2003, Vista), Exchange 2007, Operations Manager 2007, and other new systems from Microsoft. The tool allows you to use PowerShell's rich capabilities in a familiar and intuitive GUI console.

PowerShell Analyzer (http://www.powershellanalyzer.com/)
> This is an integrated development environment that focuses on leveraging PowerShell as a dynamic language. Its goal is simply to allow users to be as productive as possible in sculpting, running, interpreting results, and refactoring everything from the "one-liners" PowerShell is famous for to fully fledged, production-quality scripts.

Professional PowerShell Script Editor (http://powerwf.com/products/powerse.aspx) (PowerSE)
> PowerSE is an advanced IDE console and has all the features you've come to expect from a professional editor. It supports color syntax highlighting, IntelliSense (PowerShell, WMI, and .NET), tab completion, context-sensitive Help, and much more.

PrimalScript (http://www.sapien.com/software/primalscript)
> No matter what your role is—system, database, or network administrator; web developer; or end user developer—you probably need to work with multiple technologies, languages, and file formats at the same time. Take charge of your script development regardless of what language you use and combine PrimalScript's powerful editing and packaging abilities with your scripting skills.

PowerShell Plus (http://www.idera.com/PowerShell/powershell-plus/)
> This is the advanced PowerShell development environment. With it, you can learn PowerShell fast using the Interactive Learning Center; run PowerShell commands with the powerful interactive console; debug PowerShell 10 times faster with the advanced script editor; execute scripts remotely using customized configurations;

access hundreds of preloaded scripts in the QuickClick library; search and download thousands of community scripts; and enable team collaboration using Source Control integration.

There are other editors out there that have powerful capabilities and are highly customizable to your needs.

Vim

Short for "*Vi improved*," Vim is an advanced text editor that seeks to augment the power of the de facto Unix editor Vi with a more complete feature set. Download Vim here: *http://www.vim.org/index.php*. You can also download default syntax coloring for Windows PowerShell here: *http://www.vim.org/scripts/script.php ?script_id=1327*.

Notepad++

This is a free (as in "free speech" and also as in "free beer") source code editor and Notepad replacement that supports several languages. You can download Notepad ++ here: *http://notepad-plus-plus.org/*.

This is a sampling of what is available to you for editing, running, and debugging PowerShell scripts. Each has options out of the box and different levels of customizability.

Experiment and enjoy!

PowerShell and Visual Studio

Visual Studio is a development environment for C# programmers used to create consoles. It is also used to develop graphical user interface (GUI) applications, along with Windows Forms applications, websites, web applications, and web services. These are developed in both native and managed code for all platforms supported by Microsoft Windows, Windows Mobile, Windows CE, and .NET Framework.

Since you can embed PowerShell in a C# application—see Chapter 5—both Microsoft and PowerShell MVPs have written PowerShell consoles that work directly in and with Visual Studio:

NuGet

This is a free, open source, developer-focused, package management system for the .NET platform intent on simplifying the process of incorporating third-party libraries into a .NET application during development. NuGet also comes with a PowerShell console that runs inside Visual Studio. Download NuGet here: *http:// nuget.codeplex.com/*.

StudioShell

StudioShell is written and maintained by Jim Christopher, PowerShell MVP, on CodePlex at *http://studioshell.codeplex.com/*. If you've ever implemented a Visual Studio extension, such as an add-in or a package, you know how convoluted this space has become. You have to become an expert in your tooling if you want to change it. StudioShell changes this landscape by exposing many of Visual Studio's extensibility points in a simple and consistent way. It makes the Visual Studio IDE interactive and discoverable.

The PowerShell Community

PowerShell has a thriving community, offering open source projects and script repositories, forums, and even a PowerShell magazine. If you wondering where to get started, have a question, or want to know if someone else has already created a tool you need, these are the places to check. Plus, you can get a look at some advanced uses of PowerShell and contribute solutions based on ones that already exist.

CodePlex
> Search CodePlex for PowerShell (*http://bit.ly/KMSAWk*), and you will find that there are over 450 open source projects—and that number is growing. Here you'll find everything from tools that bring features from the UNIX world to Azure management cmdlets, testing frameworks, SQL Server integration scripts, Facebook and Twitter integration, and so much more.

PoShCode.org
> The PowerShell Code Repository (*http://poshcode.org/*) is maintained by a PowerShell MVP, Joel "Jaykul" Bennett.

PowershellCommunity.org (http://powershellcommunity.org/)
> This is a community-run and vendor-sponsored organization that provides evangelism for all things PowerShell through news, forums, user group outreach, script repository, and other resources.

PowerShell Magazine
> I am a cofounder and editor of *PowerShell Magazine* (*http://www.powershellmaga zine.com/*), along with four other great guys and PowerShell MVPs: Ravikanth Chaganti, Aleksandar Nikolić, Shay Levy, and Steven Murawski.

> Check out the site, submit an article, or just enjoy the targeted PowerShell content from some of the best scripters in the community.

Many of us in the PowerShell community are also on the forums, answering questions on StackOverflow (search "powershell"), and involved on Twitter (*#powershell*).

The Future of PowerShell on Windows 8

As mentioned in Chapter 1, Jeffrey Snover, a creator of PowerShell, wrote the *Monad Manifesto* (*http://bit.ly/9uyHlY*) in 2002 (remember, Monad was the code name for PowerShell). PowerShell was released as a separate download in 2006. Three years later, in 2009, PowerShell debuted as part of the Windows 7 operating system. A few hundred million copies of Windows 7 have been licensed in the years since its release, meaning there are a few hundred million copies of PowerShell out there, installed and ready to go.

In 2012, Windows 8 will be delivered with PowerShell v3. In addition, Windows Server 2012 will also be released. PowerShell v3 has numerous enhancements across the entire product, shipping with hundreds more PowerShell cmdlets for the client, and in the case of Windows Server 2012, over 2,300 cmdlets.

And as if this growth were not impressive enough, Microsoft is not the only company delivering PowerShell-enabled software. VMware, Cisco, Intel, Citrix, and SPLUNK, just to name a few, are doing so as well.

Summary

We've barely covered the basics here. There is an entire ocean of PowerShell awaiting us, and that's not including third-party PowerShell systems, community-delivered scripts, or the internal Microsoft teams outfitting their products.

You could say PowerShell is about 10 years old, maybe a little older, measuring from the publication of the *Monad Manifesto*. The team that developed PowerShell drew inspiration from systems developed over 30+ years ago in DEC and IBM. PowerShell is as programmable as Perl, Python, and Ruby and takes it cues from UNIX shells.

In addition, the community is thriving, which is a fundamental component to any new language and approach. Microsoft has over 50 PowerShell MVPs worldwide, providing feedback to the Microsoft PowerShell team as well as the other teams who are developing cmdlets and surfacing their APIs for easy consumption in PowerShell.

Jeffrey Snover has said, "If you're planning on working with Microsoft systems for the next year, invest some time with PowerShell—it'll make your life simpler." In the next chapters, we'll take his advice and dive a little deeper into this powerful platform.

## CHAPTER 3

The Dime Tour

*Scripting and system programming are symbiotic. Used
together, they produce programming environments of
exceptional power.*

—John Ousterhout, creator of Tcl

PowerShell provides rapid turnaround during development for a number of reasons. It
eliminates compile time, it's an interpreter and makes development more flexible by
allowing programming during application runtime, and it sits on top of powerful components, all connected by the .NET framework.

If you want to write PowerShell scripts, you need to learn the PowerShell syntax and
its building blocks—like cmdlets and functions—and how to tap into PowerShell's
ecosystem, including the .NET Framework, third-party DLLs, and DLLs you create.

There's a lot to cover, even in the dime tour, so let's get started.

The Object Pipeline: The Game Changer

These 63 characters are what hooked me when I saw my first PowerShell demo:

```
Get-Process | Where {$_.Handles -gt 750} | Sort PM -Descending
```

Handles	NPM(K)	PM(K)	WS(K)	VM(M)	CPU(s)	Id	ProcessName
965	43	173992	107044	602	157.34	2460	MetroTwit
784	21	88196	83588	290	19.84	5776	chrome
952	44	39456	20100	287	29.27	2612	explorer
784	34	34268	2836	109	4.56	3712	SearchIndexer
1158	28	18868	14048	150	6.21	956	svchost
779	14	3784	3900	36	4.46	580	lsass

This object pipeline conveys key concepts in PowerShell's value proposition: maxi-
mizing effort and reducing time. Here are the highlights:

- Using cmdlets (Get-Process, Where, Sort) to compose solutions.

- Piping .NET objects, not just text.

- Eliminating parsing and praying. No need to count spaces, tabs, and other white-space to pull out the `Handles` value and then convert it to numeric for the comparison.

- Working with .NET properties directly: `$_.Handles` in the `Where` and `PM` in the `Sort`.

- Making code less brittle. If someone adds properties to the output of `Get-Process`, my code is not affected. I am working with an object-oriented pipeline.

Automation References

When you create a console application project in Visual Studio, the wizard adds these `using` statements for you:

```
using System;
using System.Collections.Generic;
using System.Linq;
using System.Text;
```

In a PowerShell session—which you start by launching the console or integrated scripting environment (ISE)—PowerShell does more work for you. By default, there is a lot available to you in a single PowerShell session. Later, I'll cover how to import DLLs that are not included by using the `Add-Type` cmdlet or the .NET Framework directly using `[Reflection.Assembly]::Load*`.

Because ISE is a WPF application, when you load it, you'll have access to more DLLs and namespaces like the `PresentationCore`, `PresentationFramework`, and `WindowsBase`. This is a PowerShell snippet I used to print out what DLLs are referenced:

```
[System.AppDomain]::CurrentDomain.GetAssemblies() |
    Where {$_.location} |
    ForEach { Split-Path -Leaf $_.location } |
    Sort
```

The results of this snippet are as follows:

```
Microsoft.CSharp.dll
Microsoft.Management.Infrastructure.dll
Microsoft.PowerShell.Commands.Management.dll
Microsoft.PowerShell.Commands.Utility.dll
Microsoft.PowerShell.ConsoleHost.dll
Microsoft.PowerShell.Security.dll
mscorlib.dll
System.Configuration.Install.dll
System.Core.dll
System.Data.dll
System.DirectoryServices.dll
System.dll
System.Dynamic.dll
System.Management.Automation.dll
System.Management.dll
```

```
System.Numerics.dll
System.Transactions.dll
System.Xml.dll
```

PowerShell includes these automatically, so you are ready to go when you launch the console or editor.

Semicolons

Semicolons are optional. I don't use them in my scripts—too much noise and typing. They are perfectly legal though, and coming from C#, you might find it hard to lose that muscle memory of adding them.

```
PS C:\> $s = "Hello";
PS C:\> $s += " World"; $s += "!";
PS C:\> $s;
Hello World!
```

I do use them on the command line when I have multiple statements:

```
PS C:\> clear; dir *.cs
```

The good news is that if you copy and paste C# code, tweak it, and forget the semicolon, the PowerShell code will still run.

Use them if you like; I prefer less typing and thus go without.

Return Statements

Return statements are optional, too. I briefly ran a PowerShell script club in New York City. James Brundage, founder of Start-Automating (*http://start-automating.com/*), created the idea of the script club while he was on the PowerShell team and ramping up other groups in Microsoft. One of the club rules is *write only the script you need, no more*.

So, while this is correct:

```
function SayHello ($p) {
    return "Hello $p"
}

SayHello World
```

this is preferred:

```
function SayHello ($p) {
    "Hello $p"
}

SayHello World
```

There will be plenty of times when you do return in a function because it short-circuits the execution of the script at that point. But remember: when using a dynamic language like PowerShell, it is *ceremony vs. essence*. Prefer essence.

Datatypes

Datatypes are also optional. In the following example, $a = "Hello" is the same as var a = "Hello"; in C#. Each environment recognizes the variable as a string.

```
$a = "Hello"
$a # Prints Hello
$a = 1
$a += 1
$a # Prints 2
$a = 1,2,3,"a" # Create an array of different types

[int]$a = "Hello" # Error: Cannot convert value "Hello" to type "System.Int32".
```

PowerShell reduces your typing by not requiring you to explicitly define the type of variables (another example of privileging essence over ceremony). This is a significant time saver and handy when you are trying to plow through some quick prototypes on your own. When you need to take it to a more formal level—for example, sharing your script with someone else or putting your script into production—you can strongly type your variables, and this feature is at your fingertips. Passing a string to either parameter throws an error, which can be caught.

```
function Do-PrecisionCalculation {
    param (
        [Double]$Latitude,
        [Double]$Longitude
    )

    [Math]::Sin($Latitude) * [Math]::Sin($Longitude)
}
```

Exception Handling

PowerShell supports try/catch/finally, which should feel familiar to .NET developers. PowerShell v1 introduced the trap statement, which still works, but I prefer try/catch/finally.

Break

Here, I'll use the PowerShell trap statement to trap the error and stop execution of the script using the break statement.

```
trap {"trapped: $($error[0])"; break}
1/0
"done"
```

Results:

```
trapped: Attempted to divide by zero.
Attempted to divide by zero.
At line:3 char:1
+ 1/0
+ ~~~
    + CategoryInfo          : NotSpecified: (:) [], ParentContainsErrorRecordException
    + FullyQualifiedErrorId : RuntimeException
```

Continue

Here is the same `trap` example, except I'll use the `continue` statement. We should see "done" printed.

```
trap {"trapped: $($error[0])"; continue}
1/0
"done"
```

Results:

```
trapped: Attempted to divide by zero.
done
```

Try/Catch/Finally

```
try {
    1/0
    "Hello World"
} catch {
    "Error caught: $($error[0])"
} finally {
    "Finally, Hello World"
}
```

Results:

```
Error caught: Attempted to divide by zero.
Finally, Hello World
```

Quoting Rules

The following code demonstrates quoting rules in PowerShell. One key item I want to dial in on here is that the backtick (`) is the escape—not the backslash (\).

The backslash is still the escape character for regular expressions, and PowerShell does support .NET regexes.

```
"A string"
A string
```

```
"A string with 'Quotes'"
A string with 'Quotes'

"A string with `"Escaped Quotes`""
A string with "Escaped Quotes"

$s = "PowerShell"
"A string with a variable: $s"
A string with a variable: PowerShell

"A string with a quoted variable: '$s'"
A string with a quoted variable: 'PowerShell'

'Variables are not replaced inside single quotes: $s'
Variables are not replaced inside single quotes: $s
```

PowerShell Subexpressions in Strings

By using the subexpression notation, you can include arbitrary expressions in expand-able strings. A *subexpression* is a fragment of PowerShell script code that's replaced by the value resulting from the evaluation of that code.

```
$process = (Get-Process)[0]

$process.PM        # Prints 31793152
"$process.PM"      # System.Diagnostics.Process (AddInProcess32).PM
"$($process.PM)"   # Prints 31793152
```

Your mileage will vary; the PM property will have a different value on your system. The key here is that if you do not wrap $process.PM in a subexpression $(...), you'll get a result you'd never expect.

Here-Strings

Here-strings are a way to specify blocks of string literals. They preserve the line breaks and other whitespace, including indentation, in the text. They also allow variable sub-stitution and command substitution inside the string. Here-strings follow the quoting rules outlined earlier.

Great Code Generation Techniques

In the following block of string literals, I show how single and double quotes can be printed. I also embed a variable $name that gets expanded.

 I set $name outside of the HereString to World.

```
$name = "World"

$HereString = @"
This is a here-string
It can contain multiple lines
"Quotes don't need to be escaped"
Plus, you can include variables 'Hello $name'
"@
```

This is the here-string output:

```
This is a here-string
It can contain multiple lines
"Quotes don't need to be escaped"
Plus, you can include variables 'Hello World'
```

C# Code

Here-strings make code generation easier and more readable. I can copy a snippet of C#, paste it into the here-string, drop in some variables for substitution, and I'm off to the races.

```
$methodName = "Test"
$code = @"
public void $methodName()
{
    System.Console.WriteLine("This is from the $methodName method.");
}
"@

$code
```

Here are the results:

```
public void Test()
{
    System.Console.WriteLine("This is from the Test method.");
}
```

Closures, Functions, and Lambdas

A *closure*—also known as a *lexical closure, function closure, function value,* or *functional value*—is a PowerShell scriptblock coupled with a referencing environment for the nonlocal variables of that scriptblock. A PowerShell scriptblock allows the code to access variables outside its typical scope. Scriptblocks do not require a name and can be invoked using the call operator, &, as shown here:

```
$n = "PowerShell"
$closure = {"Hello $n"}
& $closure
Hello PowerShell
```

A scriptblock can have a name; this is called a *function*:

```
function Add5 ($num) {
    $num + 5
}

Add5 5
10
```

Or it can be anonymous (without a name), which is known as a *lambda*:

```
$add5 = {param($num) $num + 5}
& $add5 5 # The call operator works with parameters too!
10
```

Scriptblocks, Dynamic Languages, and Design Patterns

This example demonstrates one way to apply the strategy design pattern. Because PowerShell is a dynamic language, far less structure is needed to get the job done. I want to employ two strategies, both using multiplication. One uses the multiplication operator, while the other uses multiple additions. I could have named each scriptblock, thereby creating a function, like so: function CalcByMult($n,$m) {} and function Calc ByManyAdds($n,$m) {}.

```
# $sampleData is a multidimensional array
$sampleData = @(
    ,(3,4,12)
    ,(5,-5,-25)
)
# $strategies is an array of scriptblocks
$strategies =
{param($n,$m) $n*$m},
{
    param($n,$m)
    1..$n | ForEach {$result = 0} { $result += $m } {$result}
}

ForEach($dataset in $sampleData) {
    ForEach($strategy in $strategies) {
        & $strategy $dataset[0] $dataset[1]
    }
}
```

The nested ForEach loops first loop through the sample data and then through each of the strategies. On the first pass, & $strategy $Dataset[0] $Dataset[1] expands to and runs & {param($n,$m) $n*$m} 3 4. This produces the result 12. Next time through the inner loop, I'll have the same parameters, but the strategy will change to calculating the result doing multiple adds.

Arrays

A PowerShell array is your .NET `System.Array`. PowerShell makes interacting with arrays simpler. You can still work with them in the traditional way through subscripts, but you can also do much more.

It is dead simple to create arrays in PowerShell: separate the items with commas, and if they are text, wrap them in quotes.

```
$animals = "cat", "dog", "bat"
$animals.GetType()

IsPublic IsSerial Name     BaseType
-------- -------- ----     --------
True     True     Object[] System.Array

$animals

cat
dog
bat
```

Creating an Empty Array

As simple as it is to create an array with items, it is equally simple to create an empty array using @(). This is a special form of subexpression.

```
$animals = @()
$animals.Count
0
```

Adding an Array Item

You can easily add elements to an array using the += operator:

```
$animals = "cat", "dog", "bat"
$animals += "bird"
$animals

cat
dog
bat
bird
```

Retrieving an Element from an Array

You can access a specific array element in a familiar way using subscripts:

```
$animals = "cat", "dog", "bat"
$animals[1]
dog
```

Array Slicing

Array slicing is an operation that extracts certain elements from an array and returns them as a new array. We can print out the first two elements using the PowerShell range notation 0..1, or print out the last element of the array using -1.

```
$animals = "cat", "dog", "bat"

$animals[0..1]
cat
dog

$animals[-1] # Get the last element
bat
```

Finding Array Elements

You can use PowerShell comparison operators with arrays, too. Here I am searching the array for elements -ne (not equal) to cat:

```
$animals = "cat", "dog", "bat"
$animals -ne 'cat'
dog
bat
```

I use the -like operator and get wildcards:

```
$animals = "cat", "dog", "bat"
$animals -like '*a*'
cat
bat
```

Reversing an Array

Using the static method Reverse from the Array class, we can invert the elements and then print them. This is another example of the seamlessness of PowerShell and the .NET Framework:

```
$animals = "cat", "dog", "bat"
[array]::Reverse($animals)
$animals

# Prints
bat
dog
cat
```

Assigning Values to Multiple Variables in an Array

In PowerShell, you can assign values to multiple variables in a single pass. Here I take a heterogeneous array with five elements and set three variables—$FirstName, $Last Name, and $Rest—in one line. The first two variables are assigned items 0 and 1 of the array, respectively, and $Rest gets the remainder of the array—items 2, 3, and 4. $Rest is itself an array after the assignment.

```
PS C:\> $items = "Doug", "Finke", "NY", "NY", 10017
PS C:\> $FirstName, $LastName, $Rest = $items

PS C:\> $FirstName
Doug
PS C:\> $LastName
Finke
PS C:\> "$Rest"
NY NY 10017
```

Parentheses and Commas

Coming from C# to PowerShell, you'll find that parentheses require a little extra cognitive effort. They show up where you expect them: around and between parameters to a function.

```
function Test ($p, $x) {
    "This is the value of p $p and the value of x $x"
}
```

If you use parentheses when you call the function Test, you get unexpected results:

```
Test (1, 2)
This is the value of p 1 2 and the value of x
```

Here is how you revise the previous example to get the results you'd expect:

```
Test 1 2
This is the value of p 1 and the value of x 2
```

Calling Test with (1, 2) actually passes the numbers 1 and 2 as an array to the parameter $p; PowerShell unrolls that, and the string is printed.

This takes practice, but don't worry—it is absolutely worth the investment.

Hash Tables

A *hash table* or *hash map* is a data structure that lets you map keys (e.g., a person's name) to their associated values (e.g., the person's telephone number). A hash table implements an *associative array*.

Creating an Empty Hash Table

The @{} creates an empty hash table, similar to the @() used to create the empty array.

```
$h = @{}
$h.Count
0
$h.GetType()
```

```
IsPublic IsSerial Name       BaseType
-------- -------- ----       --------
True     True     Hashtable  System.Object
```

Adding a Hash Table Item

Once we have an empty hash table, we can map keys and values to it. With PowerShell, we can use either the traditional approach or dot notation:

```
$h = @{}
$h["Item0"] = 0 # More ceremony
$h.Item1 = 1 # Notice, dot notation
$h.Item2 = 2
$h # Prints the Hash table
Name  Value
----  -----
Item1 1
Item0 0
Item2 2
```

Initializing a Hash Table with Items

Here I create a hash table and two keys with values. Then, using dot notation, I print out the value of the key named Item1.

```
$h = @{Item1=1;Item2=2}
$h.Item1 # dot notation and no casting
1
```

Concatenating Hash Tables

The addition operator also works on hash tables, as well as on strings and arrays.

```
$h1 = @{a=1;b=2}
$h2 = @{c=3;d=4}

$h1+$h2

# Prints
Name Value
---- -----
d    4
c    3
b    2
a    1
```

Get-Member

Get-Member returns the members (properties and methods) of objects at the command line. It is one of the key cmdlets I use regularly. I get all of the information about an object—its type, methods, properties, events, and more—right there. When working with a script, you'll find it very handy; you can just add an `$obj | Get-Member` in the script and inspect all these details about an object you are working with.

```
1.0 | Get-Member


    TypeName: System.Double

Name          MemberType Definition
----          ---------- ----------
CompareTo     Method     int CompareTo(System.Object value)
Equals        Method     bool Equals(System.Object obj), bo
GetHashCode   Method     int GetHashCode()
GetType       Method     type GetType()
GetTypeCode   Method     System.TypeCode GetTypeCode()
ToBoolean     Method     bool ToBoolean(System.IFormatProvi
ToByte        Method     byte ToByte(System.IFormatProvider
ToChar        Method     char ToChar(System.IFormatProvider
ToDateTime    Method     System.DateTime ToDateTime(System.
ToDecimal     Method     decimal ToDecimal(System.IFormatPr
ToDouble      Method     double ToDouble(System.IFormatProv
ToInt16       Method     System.Int16 ToInt16(System.IForma
ToInt32       Method     int ToInt32(System.IFormatProvider
ToInt64       Method     long ToInt64(System.IFormatProvide
ToSByte       Method     System.SByte ToSByte(System.IForma
ToSingle      Method     float ToSingle(System.IFormatProvi
ToString      Method     string ToString(), string ToString
ToType        Method     System.Object ToType(type conversi
ToUInt16      Method     System.UInt16 ToUInt16(System.IFor
ToUInt32      Method     System.UInt32 ToUInt32(System.IFor
ToUInt64      Method     System.UInt64 ToUInt64(System.IFor
```

Filtering with Get-Member

In the preceding example, notice it tells you the type right at the top. I used a double as an example; if I had instead used a reference type, you would see properties, events, and more. With Get-Member, you can filter on MemberType, too.

```
New-Object Net.Webclient | Get-Member -MemberType Property


    TypeName: System.Net.WebClient

Name             MemberType Definition
----             ---------- ----------
BaseAddress      Property   System.String BaseAddress {get;set;}
CachePolicy      Property   System.Net.Cache.RequestCachePolicy
Container        Property   System.ComponentModel.IContainer
Credentials      Property   System.Net.ICredentials Credentials
Encoding         Property   System.Text.Encoding Encoding {get;set;}
Headers          Property   System.Net.WebHeaderCollection Headers
IsBusy           Property   System.Boolean IsBusy {get;}
Proxy            Property   System.Net.IWebProxy Proxy {get;set;}
QueryString      Property   System.Collections.Specialized.NameVal
ResponseHeaders  Property   System.Net.WebHeaderCollection ResponseHea
```

```
Site                  Property  System.ComponentModel.ISite Site {get;set;}
UseDefaultCredentials Property  System.Boolean UseDefaultCredentials {get;se
```

Using Get-Member with Collections

Here is some PowerShell magic that is useful, but sometimes not what you want:

```
$range = 1..10
$range | Get-Member
```

By piping the $range to Get-Member, PowerShell prints out the details about the different elements in the array, not the collection itself. In this case, since I used the range operator 1..10, all the elements are Int32, so I get the details about the type Int32.

```
    TypeName: System.Int32

Name       MemberType Definition
----       ---------- ----------
ToBoolean  Method     bool ToBoolean(System.IFormatProvider provid
ToByte     Method     byte ToByte(System.IFormatProvider provider)
ToChar     Method     char ToChar(System.IFormatProvider provider)
ToDateTime Method     System.DateTime ToDateTime(System.IFormatPro
ToDecimal  Method     decimal ToDecimal(System.IFormatProvider pro
ToDouble   Method     double ToDouble(System.IFormatProvider provi
```

If the $range were heterogeneous, Get-Member would return the details for each type. (To be more accurate, the PowerShell object flow engine would do that, but I won't be discussing the flow engine here.)

What if you wanted to get the details on $range though? Simple—use the -InputObject on the Get-Member cmdlet:

```
$range = 1..10
Get-Member -InputObject $range
```

Here is an edited version of what is returned about the collection $range.

```
    TypeName: System.Object[]

Name           MemberType    Definition
----           ----------    ----------
Count          AliasProperty Count = Length
Add            Method        int Add(System.Object value)
Clear          Method        System.Void Clear()
GetEnumerator  Method        System.Collections.IEnumerato
GetLowerBound  Method        int GetLowerBound(int dimensi
IndexOf        Method        int IndexOf(System.Object val
Initialize     Method        System.Void Initialize()
Insert         Method        System.Void Insert(int index,
IsReadOnly     Property      bool IsReadOnly {get;}
IsSynchronized Property      bool IsSynchronized {get;}
Length         Property      int Length {get;}
```

Looking into PowerShell cmdlets deeper, you'll often find options where piping or passing parameters—while not necessarily what you originally had in mind—yields

Figure 3-1. Injecting a GUI

the results that you want. This speaks to the cognitive shift of PowerShell and is worth the time you invest.

Inject a GUI into the PowerShell Command Line

Let's say I get too much output at the command line from `Get-Member`. No problem— let's pipe to a GUI using `Out-GridView`. `Out-GridView` comes with PowerShell, ready to go out of the box (see Figure 3-1).

```
New-Object Net.Webclient | Get-Member | Out-GridView
```

I recommend playing with `Out-GridView`. It has a filter, which subsets the list as you type. In version 3, it has a `-PassThru` parameter that lets you select items, which get passed down the pipeline when you click OK.

`Out-GridView` saves you time and effort when debugging. In a multiline script, you can add a line where you pipe a variable containing an array of objects to it and run the script, and this window pops up. `Out-GridView` is a great way to inspect what happened.

New-Object

`New-Object` creates an instance of a Microsoft .NET Framework object. In this section, I'll "new" up a component object model (COM) object and launch Internet Explorer, and then I'll new up a native PowerShell object, `PSObject`, and add properties to it. I'll then show the streamlined PowerShell v3 syntax, and finally, I'll work with a .NET Framework object.

Launching Internet Explorer

Here, in three lines of PowerShell, I can create a COM object, call a method on it, and set a property. I don't know how many lines are needed to get this done in C#. Remember the ProgID? That is how we used to interact with COM objects. Here, I am using the ProgID InternetExplorer.Application; then I'm navigating to the Google page and making IE visible. If you've got a ProgID, PowerShell can make short work of it.

```
$ie = New-Object -ComObject InternetExplorer.Application
$ie.Navigate2("http://www.google.com")
$ie.Visible = $true
```

Creating a New PowerShell Object

PSObject is the PowerShell object. It is the root of the synthetic type system in PowerShell. Here, I am creating a new one and adding two properties to it, Name and Age, and setting values to them:

```
$obj = New-Object PSObject -Property @{
    Name = "John"
    Age = 10
}

$obj.GetType()
IsPublic IsSerial Name            BaseType
-------- -------- ----            --------
True     False    PSCustomObject  System.Object

$obj
Age Name
--- ----
 10 John
```

PowerShell v3 is more pithy

Version 3 of PowerShell comes with a ton of new features. Here, I am getting the same results as the previous example, but with less typing. Less typing, more results—that's what PowerShell is all about.

```
[PSCustomObject] @{
    Name = "John"
    Age = 10
}

Name Age
---- ---
John  10
```

Using the .NET Framework

I can also instantiate .NET Framework components. This is a primary use case for a .NET developer. I use this to instantiate the components I write and deliver as DLLs.

```
$wc = New-Object Net.WebClient
[xml]$resp = $wc.DownloadString("http://feeds.feedburner.com/DevelopmentInABlink")
$resp.rss.channel.item| ForEach {$_.Title}

NumPy 1.5 Beginner's Guide
Design Patterns in Dynamic Languages-PowerShell
Using PowerShell in Roslyn's C# Interactive Window
PowerShell - Handling CSV and JSON
PowerShell for .Net Developers-A Survey
PowerShell vNext - Web Service Entities
Reading RSS Feeds-Even easier in PowerShell V3
```

Add-Member

Here I used Add-Member to extend the .NET string object and added Reverse, which reverses the letters in the string. I created a new ScriptProperty (Add-Member can add other types like NoteProperty) and in the scriptblock, I referenced the object and its properties using the $this variable.

```
$s = "Hello World" |
    Add-Member -PassThru ScriptProperty Reverse {$this[$this.Length..0] -join ""}

$s
Hello World

$s.Reverse
dlroW olleH
```

Add-Type

The Add-Type cmdlet adds a Microsoft .NET Framework type (a class) to a Windows PowerShell session. Add-Type has a few parameters I'll demonstrate in this section; for example, TypeDefinition lets me compile C# code on the fly, and it supports VB.NET. I'll also show the Path parameter, which lets me load a DLL into a PowerShell session.

Compiling C# on the Fly

In the following example, you should recognize the text inside the here-string—a.k.a. the stuff between the @""@. It is a C# MyMathClass class with a single method, Add. I am passing the here-string to the -TypeDefinition parameter, and the Add-Type cmdlet will compile it on the fly, in memory, into the current PowerShell session. If I am running a script, it compiles the code just for the life of that script.

```
Add-Type -TypeDefinition @"
public class MyMathClass {
    public int Add(int n1, int n2) {
        return n1 + n2;
    }
}
"@
```

Newing Up the Class

After compiling the C# code, I want to use it, so I use the New-Object cmdlet. This is equivalent to var obj = new MyMathClass();. From there, I print out the object's type and then use Get-Member to get the details of the object I am working with.

```
$obj = New-Object MyMathClass
$obj.GetType()

IsPublic IsSerial Name          BaseType
-------- -------- ----          --------
True     False    MyMathClass   System.Object

$obj | Get-Member

   TypeName: MyMathClass

Name        MemberType Definition
----        ---------- ----------
Add         Method     int Add(int n1, int n2)
Equals      Method     bool Equals(System.Object obj)
GetHashCode Method     int GetHashCode()
GetType     Method     type GetType()
ToString    Method     string ToString()
```

Calling the Add Method on MyMathClass

Let's exercise the newly minted code by adding the numbers 1–5 to themselves and printing them out. It's important to note here that I am not telling PowerShell how to print or loop. I don't check for the end of the stream, or end of file. It just works.

```
1..5 | ForEach {$obj.Add($_,$_)}
2
4
6
8
10
```

Wait, I Don't Have the Source

What if I didn't give you the C# source code? No problem. Use the -Path parameter and let Add-Type do the rest.

```
Add-Type -Path C:\Temp\MyMathClass.dll
```

This is similar to adding a reference to a project and then a using statement. You can apply the previous PowerShell statements for the same results.

I could also have used the .NET Framework to get the job done.

```
[Reflection.Assembly]::LoadFile("C:\Temp\MyMathClass.dll")
```

For more details, check out my blog post, "How to Load .NET Assemblies in a PowerShell Session," at *http://bit.ly/c6H1a8*.

"What Does % Do?" and Other Aliases

PowerShell has an aliasing system that allows you to create or change an alias for a cmdlet or for a command element, such as a function, a script, a file, or other executable.

So, % is aliased to ForEach, and ? is aliased to Where. These two PowerShell lines are equivalent; they find the even numbers, multiply them by 2, and print them:

```
1..10 | ? {$_ % 2 -eq 0} | % {$_*2}
1..10 | Where {$_ % 2 -eq 0} | ForEach {$_*2}
4
8
12
16
20
```

In my PowerShell profile, $PROFILE, I alias vs to the Visual Studio executable. So whenever I need to launch it, I simply type vs and press Enter:

```
Set-Alias vs
 "C:\Program Files\Microsoft Visual Studio 10.0\Common7\idc\devenv.exe"
```

Modules

PowerShell modules are fundamental to organizing your scripts. You can place your scripts in subfolders, and from the module you can recursively find them all and dot-source them into a PowerShell session. It's a fantastic way to speed development. You can just drop a script into a directory below your module (which has a *.psm1* extension), do an Import-Module –Force *module name*, and you're ready to rock.

Here is a list of modules on my box. They are probably different than yours because I have PowerShell v3 CTP2 installed on Windows 7.

```
Get-Module -ListAvailable | Select Name
AppLocker
BitsTransfer
CimCmdlets
Microsoft.PowerShell.Core
Microsoft.PowerShell.Diagnostics
Microsoft.PowerShell.Host
Microsoft.PowerShell.Management
Microsoft.PowerShell.Security
```

```
Microsoft.PowerShell.Utility
Microsoft.WSMan.Management
PSDiagnostics
PSScheduledJob
PSWorkflow
TroubleshootingPack
```

Modules are your friends. Learn them, love them, and use them. They are how Microsoft teams deliver their PowerShell functionality. Once you grow beyond a few scripts that interact, modules are the preferred packaging mechanism.

Let's say I have this script stored in a PowerShell file in my scripts directory, *C:\Scripts \MyCountScript.ps1*.

```
$count = 0
function Add-OneTocount { $count += 1 }
function Get-Count      { $count }
```

I can source this script by inputting a dot (.) followed by the fully qualified script filename, like so: `. C:\Scripts\MyCountScript.ps1`. Dot sourcing will load and run the script; variables become global, as do functions. This is good news and bad news. The good news is that it lets me rapidly iterate and problem solve. The bad news is, if I deliver this as is to a colleague or client, and he has a script he dot-sources that uses `$count`, we'll have a collision.

Modules help with scoping, but that is just the beginning of what they do (remember, this is the dime tour). I will illustrate quickly how to ramp up easily on modules. I can rename my script to *C:\Scripts\MyCountScript.psm1* (note, I only changed *ps1* to *psm1*). Now I need to "load" it, and since I cannot dot-source it I'll use `Import-Module`.

```
Import-Module C:\Scripts\MyCountScript.psm1
```

That's it! Now `$count` is not visible outside of the module, and we are safe.

As mentioned, there's a lot more to modules, but again, the main thing is to *learn them, love them, and use them*.

Summary

OK, that's the end of the dime tour. We took a nice swim across the surface, dipped under for a couple of feet, and had a bit of a deep dive. Remember, PowerShell v2 had a couple hundred cmdlets, PowerShell v3 over 400, and Windows Server 2012 delivers over 2,300. That's a lot of good stuff, and it doesn't even include PowerShell remoting, background jobs, Windows Workflow, idiomatic aspects, best practices, tips and tricks, and so much more.

PowerShell requires your investment. The good news is that you can become very productive very quickly by just learning some basics. When you're ready to develop your PowerShell skills further, you'll benefit by using it to support your development process, deliver more powerful products, make your product more manageable, and deliver faster and better functionality, all while enabling system integrators and end users to generate custom solutions based on software you're providing.

Want to know how? Read on.

## CHAPTER 4

Accelerating Delivery

In this chapter we'll work through different types of text extraction and manipulation. This functionality ties into creating code generators, which take over the task of writing repetitive infrastructure code, thereby eliminating grunt work. PowerShell's ability to work in this way—reading text, XML, and DLL metadata—enables productivity and consistency while driving up the quality of the deliverable.

Being able to rip through numerous source code files looking for text in a specific context and extracting key information is super useful; primarily, it means we can locate key information quickly. Plus, because we can generate a .NET object with properties, we can easily pipe the results and do more work easily. For example, we can:

- Export the results to a CSV and do analysis on them with Excel.
- Catalog strings for use by QA/QC.
- Create lists of classes, methods, and functions.

Let's get started exploring this useful and timesaving functionality.

Scanning for const Definitions

The examples in this section read C# files looking for strings containing the word const, extracting the variable name and value. Scanning for strings across files takes many forms—searching SQL files, PowerShell scripts, JavaScript files, and HTML files, just to name a few. Once the information is extracted, you can use it again in many ways—for example, cataloging strings for internationalization, analyzing code, creating indexes of class methods and functions, and locating global variables. The list goes on and on.

```
public const int Name = "Dog";
const double Freezing = 32;
```

This reader will look for const definitions in C# files like the previous one and produce the following output:

```
FileName Name     Value
-------- ----     -----
test1.cs Name     "Dog"
test1.cs Freezing 32
```

I will show two versions of the code. The first will read a single file, and the second will search a directory for all C# files and process them. Both examples are nearly identical, differing only in how I work with the `Select-String` cmdlet.

Reading a Single C# File

This is an example of a single C# file, *test.cs*. It has three `const` variables defined—two scoped at the class level and one at the method level.

```
using System;
using System.Collections.Generic;
using System.Linq;
using System.Text;

namespace ConsoleApplication1
{
    class Program
    {
        public const string Test = "test";
        public const int TestX = 1;

        static void Main(string[] args)
        {
            const double PI = 3.14;
        }
    }
}
```

Next up, we'll cover the PowerShell script to scan and extract the `const` pattern.

Using Select-String

It's import to note that we are doing pattern matching here, not parsing. If one of these lines of code is in a comment, this reader will find it because it cannot tell the difference between a comment and a "real" line of code.

The reader will find these `const` definitions and then output them in this format. This is an array of PowerShell objects, each having three properties: `FileName`, `Name`, and `Value`.

```
$regex = "\s+const\s+\w+\s+(?<name>.*)\s+=\s+(?<value>.*);"

Select-String $regex .\test.cs |
    ForEach {
        $fileName = $_.Path
        ForEach($match in $_.Matches) {
            New-Object PSObject -Property @{
                FileName = $fileName
```

```
                     Name      = $match.Groups["name"].Value
                     Value     = $match.Groups["value"].Value
                  }
               }
            }
```

Here is the result:

```
    FileName Name  Value
    -------- ----  -----
    test.cs  Test  "test"
    test.cs  TestX 1
    test.cs  PI    3.14
```

Select-String finds text in files or strings. For UNIX folks, this is equivalent to grep. In this example, we are using a regular expression with the named groups "name" and "value". Select-String can also find text using the –SimpleMatch keyword, meaning Select-String will not interpret the pattern as a regular expression statement.

So, the parameters we're passing are the pattern and filename. If matches are found, they are piped to a ForEach. We capture the $fileName from the property $_.Path ($_ is the current item in the pipeline) and then pipe the matches ($_.Matches) to another ForEach. In the ForEach we create a new PSObject on the fly with three properties, FileName, Name, and Value. Where did Name and Value come from? They came from the named groups in the regular expression.

We extracted data and created a custom output type using Select-String and New-Object PSObject. We can rip through any text-based file, searching for information, and then present it as a .NET object with properties. We could have even piped this data to Export-Csv .\MyFile.CSV, which converts it to comma-separated values (CSV) and saves it to a file. Then we could do an Invoke-Item .\MyFile.CSV, opening the file in Excel, parsed and ready to go.

Reading C# Files in a Directory

In this example, we use Select-String again. The difference is we're doing a dir for files ending in .cs and then piping them to Select-String. From there, the process is the same as before.

```
$regex = "\s+const\s+\w+\s+(?<name>.*)\s+=\s+(?<value>.*);"

dir *.cs | Select-String $regex |
    ForEach {
        $fileName = $_.Path
        ForEach($match in $_.Matches) {
            New-Object PSObject -Property @{
                FileName = $fileName
                Name      = $match.Groups["name"].Value
                Value     = $match.Groups["value"].Value
            }
        }
    }
```

Here is the result:

```
FileName Name     Value
-------- ----     -----
test.cs  Test     "test"
test.cs  TestX    1
test.cs  PI       3.14
test1.cs Color    "Red"
test1.cs Name     "Dog"
test1.cs Freezing 32
```

PowerShell simplifies the process of traversing directories to search for patterns in the text and transforming the results into objects with properties. We could further pipe these results to other PowerShell built-in cmdlets or to our own functions in order to do all kinds of work for us.

Consider refactoring this script by varying either the regex or files you want to search for, but keeping the same type of output.

This is a two-foot dive into what you can do using PowerShell's `Select-String`, regular expressions, and objects with properties. There is an entire ocean of possibilities you can apply this extraction technique to with text files. Once the strings have been extracted and are in the form of a list of PowerShell objects, you can generate a wide variety of output, including HTML documentation and many other programmatic elements.

Working with Template Engines

A *template engine* is software that is designed to process templates and content to produce output documents. Writing a simple template engine in PowerShell is straightforward. This approach lets us write many different types of templates in text and then leverage PowerShell to dynamically generate a file's content based on variables or more complex logic.

The Engine

Template engines typically include features common to most high-level programming languages, with an emphasis on features for processing plain text. Such features include:

- Variables and functions
- Text replacement
- File inclusion
- Conditional evaluation and loops

Because we are using PowerShell to write the engine, we not only get all these benefits, but we can also use all of PowerShell's features, cmdlets, and functionality.

The parameter $ScriptBlock is the script block we'll pass in a later example. To execute it, we use the & (call operator). Invoke-Template supports the keyword Get-Template. We define this keyword simply by creating a function named Get-Template. Here we nest that function inside the Invoke-Template function. Get-Template take one parameter, $TemplateFileName.

```
function Invoke-Template {
    param(
        [string]$Path,
        [Scriptblock]$ScriptBlock
    )

    function Get-Template {
        param($TemplateFileName)

        $content = [IO.File]::ReadAllText(
            (Join-Path $Path $TemplateFileName) )
        Invoke-Expression "@`"`r`n$content`r`n`"@"
    }

    & $ScriptBlock
}
```

In essence, this example has three moving parts: the execution of the script block, which calls Get-Template; the reading of that file's contents, using the .NET Framework's System.IO.File.ReadAllText static method; and finally, PowerShell's Invoke-Expression, which evaluates the content just read as though it were a here-string.

Notice how Invoke-Template takes a -ScriptBlock as a second parameter. Practically speaking, Invoke-Template is an internal *domain-specific language* (DSL), meaning we have the entire PowerShell ecosystem available to us and can get really creative inside this script block, calling cmdlets, getting templates, and generating code. This opens the door for lots of automation possibilities, saving us time and effort and reducing defects in our deliverables.

A Single Variable

Let's use the template engine in a simple example. I set up this template in a file called *TestHtml.htm* in the subdirectory *etc*.

```
<h1>Hello $name</h1>
```

We use an HTML tag plus PowerShell syntax to define the variable for replacement, $name. Here are contents of the *TestHtml.htm*. Note, this is the verbose version. We explicitly specify the parameter names –Path, -ScriptBlock, and -TemplateName.

```
# dot-source it
. .\Invoke-Template.ps1

Invoke-Template -Path "$pwd\etc" -ScriptBlock {
    $name = "World"
```

```
    Get-Template -TemplateFileName TestHtml.htm
}
```

Here's the terse approach, letting PowerShell bind the parameters:

```
# dot-source it
. .\Invoke-Template.ps1

Invoke-Template "$pwd\etc" {
    $name = "World"
    Get-Template TestHtml.htm
}
```

While the intent of code is clearer using named parameters, I prefer less typing and typically write my code as terse as possible. Both versions are valid because of PowerShell's parameter binding.

Here is our result:

```
<h1>Hello World</h1>
```

Multiple Variables

Expanding on the theme of variable replacement, we'll replace two variables. The template is a blend of C# and PowerShell variables; after the variable replacement, it'll be a C# property.

```
public $type $name {get; set;}
```

And now, the script:

```
Invoke-Template "$pwd\etc" {
    $type = "string"
    $name = "FirstName"
    Get-Template properties.txt
}
```

Invoke-Template stitches the variables and template together, and I think it is important to extrapolate here. You can have any number of Invoke-Template calls in a single script, each pointing to a different filepath for its set of templates. Plus, the code inside the script block can be far more involved in setting up numerous variables and calling Get-Template multiple times, pulling in any number of templates.

Here is our result:

```
public string FirstName {get; set;}
```

Multiple Templates

Say we want to create both public and private C# variables. We do this by calling different templates. In this example, I am demoing multiple templates. I want to create two properties, a string FirstName and a DateTime Date. For the Date property though,

I want a get and a `private set`. I create a file in the *etc* directory called *privateSet.txt* and stub what I want to generate.

Here are the contents of *Test-MultipleVariableTemplate.ps1*:

```
# dot-source it
. .\Invoke-Template.ps1

Invoke-Template "$pwd\etc" {

    $type = "string"
    $name = "FirstName"
    Get-Template properties.txt

    $type = "DateTime"
    $name = "Date"
    Get-Template privateSet.txt
}
```

This is incredibly useful; for example, we can write PowerShell code that reads the schema of a SQL table, grabs the column names and datatypes, and generates an entire C# class that maps our table to an object. Yes, there are other tools that do this, but just a few lines of PowerShell will handle these key processes and give you control of the entire workflow. Plus, most off-the-shelf products can't always give us fine-grained control over the acquisition, processing, and output of the results. There are always exceptions.

Here is our result:

```
public string FirstName {get; set;}
public DateTime Date {get; private set;}
```

This is just a small sampling of what is possible with `Invoke-Template`. It's a very powerful way to organize simple text replacement and get a lot done. Now let's move on to some more involved scripts.

Complex Logic

In this example, we're using the built-in `Import-Csv` cmdlet to read a CSV (comma-separated value) file.

```
Type, Name
string, LastName
int, Age
```

Here, we're piping the contents of the CSV to `ForEach`, setting the appropriate variables, and finally calling the template *properties.txt*.

```
Invoke-Template "$pwd\etc" {
    Import-Csv $pwd\properties.csv | ForEach {
        $type = $_.Type
        $name = $_.Name
        Get-Template properties.txt
```

```
        }
    }
```

Here is our result:

```
public string LastName {get; set;}
public int Age {get; set;}
```

The template is the same as the previous example, and the PowerShell script to create it is nearly identical, the main difference being that the input here is from a CSV file.

We can continue to add properties to the CSV file, rerun the script, and code generate as many C# properties as we need. With a little creativity, we might view this as a first step in code generating an entire C# class, ready for compilation.

UML Style Syntax

To demonstrate how flexible PowerShell is, I created a file containing properties in UML syntax and then used the built-in PowerShell cmdlet Import-Csv to read the file and convert it to an array of PowerShell objects, each having the properties Name and Type. By default, Import-Csv reads the first line and uses it to name the properties. I override that by specifying Name and Type in the -Header property. I also override the default delimiter ",", setting the -Delimiter property to ":".

```
LastName  : string
FirstName : string
Age       : int
City      : string
State     : string
Zip       : int


. .\Invoke-Template.ps1

Invoke-Template "$pwd\etc" {
    Import-Csv -Path .\Uml.txt -Header "Name","Type" -Delimiter ":" |
        ForEach {
            $name = $_.Name
            $type = $_.Type
            Get-Template properties.txt
        }
}
```

With a little imagination, you can work up a number of interesting, useful formats that make it simple to represent information and then transform it into many other types of output.

Here is our result:

```
public string LastName  {get; set;}
public string FirstName {get; set;}
public int Age {get; set;}
public string City  {get; set;}
public string State  {get; set;}
public int Zip {get; set;}
```

Reading XML

PowerShell is not limited to reading CSV files, so we have options. As a developer, I use XML as a part of my daily diet. Here, I'll play off the previous example of generating C# properties, this time using XML to drive the input to the process.

```
<properties>
    <property>
        <type>string</type>
        <name>City</name>
    </property>
    <property>
        <type>string</type>
        <name>State</name>
    </property>
    <property>
        <type>string</type>
        <name>Zip</name>
    </property>
</properties>
```

Let's read the XML and convert it:

```
Invoke-Template "$pwd\etc" {
    ([xml](Get-Content .\Properties.xml)).properties.property |
        ForEach {
            $type = $_.type
            $name = $_.name
            Get-Template properties.txt
        }
}
```

This is the same script as the complex logic version in the previous example, but instead of reading from a CSV file with `Import-Csv`, we now read the file using `Get-Content`, applying the PowerShell `[xml]` accelerator and dot notation over the nodes.

Here is the result:

```
public string City {get; set;}
public string State {get; set;}
public string Zip {get; set;}
```

There it is—the transformation of XML data into C #properties. The separation of the text being replaced from the PowerShell that processes the input really highlights the essence of using PowerShell. This handful of scripts processes and transforms information into very *readable* and *maintainable C#*.

Bonus Round

Next we'll invoke all three scripts one after the other. The PowerShell engine takes care of handling the output from all of them. We're bringing together information from three disparate sources.

```
.\Test-MultipleVariableTemplate.ps1
.\Test-ComplexLogicTemplate.ps1
.\Test-ReadXMLTemplate.ps1
```

We can easily pipe this to *Set-Content Person.cs*, and we are well on our way to generating code that compiles. Here's the result:

```
public string FirstName {get; set;}
public string LastName {get; set;}
public int Age {get; set;}
public string City {get; set;}
public string State {get; set;}
public string Zip {get; set;}
```

Using template engines and PowerShell, we have tremendous reach. We can pull information from numerous sources—a database, Excel, a web service, or a web page, just to name a few. Plus, we can call Get-Template multiple times in the same script, each instance pointing to different templates, and produce a number of different outputs.

Generating PowerShell Functions from C# Methods

Next, we're going to compile a C# class, MyMath, on the fly, using the built-in Add-Type cmdlet. Note, Add-Type also lets us load either a DLL or C# source file. Now we have a new type, MyMath, loaded in our PowerShell session. We can use the methods on the .NET Framework's System.Type class, like GetMethods(), on this type to get information.

```
$code = @"
    public class MyMath
    {
        public int  MyAdd(int n1, int n2)      { return n1 + n2; }
        public int  MySubtract(int n1, int n2) { return n1 - n2; }
        public int  MyMultiply(int n1, int n2) { return n1 * n2; }
        public int  MyDivide(int n1, int n2)   { return n1 / n2; }
        public void MyTest() {System.Console.WriteLine("Test");}
    }
"@

Add-Type -TypeDefinition $code
```

Here we take the output of GetMethods() and display it in a GUI using Out-GridView (see Figure 4-1).

```
[MyMath].GetMethods() | Where {$_.Name -like "My*"} | Out-GridView
```

As you know, PowerShell is based on .NET, so here we tap into the framework and use GetMethods() on the type MyMath. First, we'll create the variable $code to hold our C# class and its methods. Then, Add-Type will compile the code in the current PowerShell session. Lastly, we use brackets [] around the name of our class MyMath, indicating to PowerShell that it is a type, and then we can call GetMethods(). I frequently use this approach when working with C# code/DLLs at the command line. I have used the

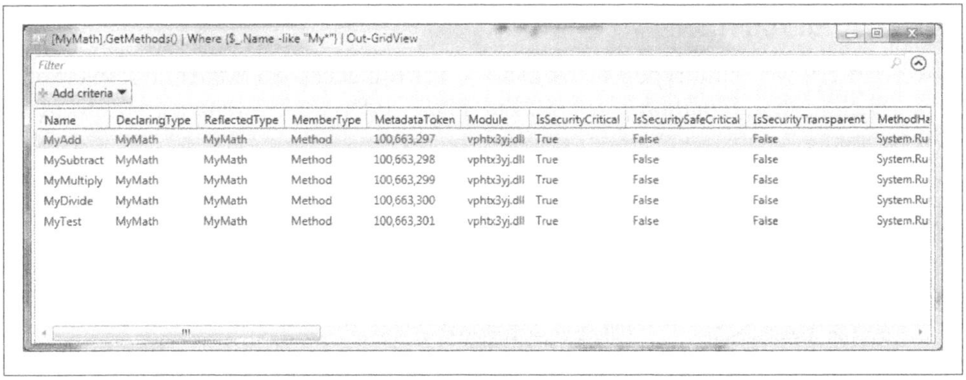

Figure 4-1. Inject a GUI in your pipeline—showing methods on a C# object

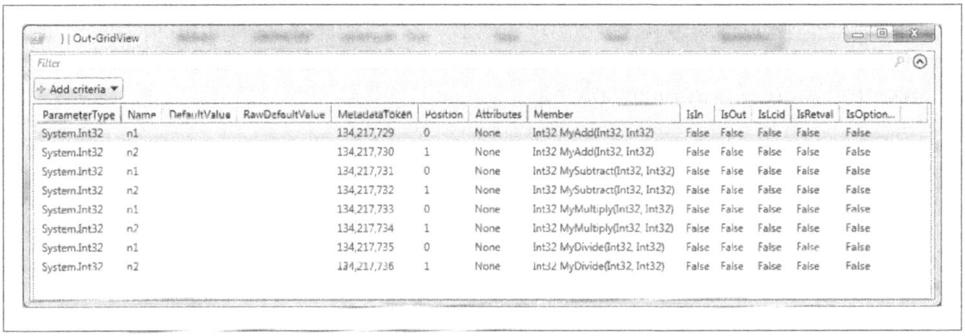

Figure 4-2. Showing C# parameters from method signatures

"long form" of the code in the script example for clarity. When I do this at the command line, I like the pithy version better because it saves time, effort, and keystrokes.

In PowerShell v3, it gets simpler—cleaner, less noise, fewer keystrokes, and more essence. Here the Where syntax loses the curly braces, and the $_ :

```
[MyMath].GetMethods() | Where Name -like "My*" | Out-GridView
```

Get Parameters

Now we'll take the last line of PowerShell from the previous example and pipe it to ForEach, calling the .NET GetParameters() method. Then we'll pipe it to Out-Grid View and get a nice summary of parameter information on MyMath code implementation, as shown in Figure 4-2.

```
[MyMath].GetMethods() | Where {$_.Name -like "My*"} |
    ForEach {
        $_.GetParameters()
    } | Out-GridView
```

Pulling It All Together

If we wanted, we could type this by hand to get full access to `MyMath` in PowerShell. PowerShell is an *automation platform*; I'm a lazy coder, so I'll write a script to make that happen.

```
$MyMath = New-Object MyMath

function Invoke-MyAdd ($n1, $n2) {$MyMath.MyAdd($n1, $n2)}
function Invoke-MySubtract ($n1, $n2) {$MyMath.MySubtract($n1, $n2)}
function Invoke-MyMultiply ($n1, $n2) {$MyMath.MyMultiply($n1, $n2)}
function Invoke-MyDivide ($n1, $n2) {$MyMath.MyDivide($n1, $n2)}
function Invoke-MyTest () {$MyMath.MyTest()}
```

Wrapping `MyMath` in PowerShell functions is a gateway to many capabilities. For example, we can interact with `MyMath` at the command line or in scripts, write tests, and pipe results to the rest of the PowerShell ecosystem. PowerShell enables us to compose code in ways we can't in a system language like C#. In this simple example, I let PowerShell handle parameters through parameter binding so I can focus less on mechanics and more on problem solving:

```
Invoke-MyAdd 1 3
1..10 |
    ForEach {Invoke-MyAdd $_ $_} |
    ForEach {Invoke-MyMultiply $_ $_}
```

I've shown PowerShell code that can get the methods and parameters for an object that is loaded into a PowerShell session. The next script will combine these, and using a here-string, will create the PowerShell functions that fully wrap `MyMath` signatures in a PowerShell way.

One line gets a bit funky, however. In the `Get-Parameter` function, I have "`` `$$ ``($_.Name)"; this is needed in order to generate the $n1. I use the PowerShell escape character ` before the first $; otherwise, PowerShell would interpret that as $$. That is a PowerShell automatic variable, which contains the last token in the last line received. The $($_.Name) is a subexpression, and is a simple rule to memorize when you want to expand variables in strings.

```
function Get-Parameter ($target) {
    ($target.GetParameters() |
        ForEach {
            "`$$($_.Name)"
        }
    ) -join ", "
}

@"
`$MyMath = New-Object MyMath
$([MyMath].GetMethods() | Where {$_.Name -like "My*"} | ForEach {

    $params = Get-Parameter $_

@"
```

```
function Invoke-$($_.Name) ($params) {`$MyMath.$($_.Name)($($params))}
"@
})

"@
```

Generating PowerShell wrappers is a scalable approach, as compared to manually transforming the C# method signatures to PowerShell functions. In addition, if our C# code is still changing, we have a single script solution to wrapping our C# functions and make them PowerShell ready. Again, this saves us time and effort, and we'll have fewer finger errors.

Here is our result:

```
function Invoke-MyAdd ($n1, $n2) {$MyMath.MyAdd($n1, $n2)}
function Invoke-MySubtract ($n1, $n2) {$MyMath.MySubtract($n1, $n2)}
function Invoke-MyMultiply ($n1, $n2) {$MyMath.MyMultiply($n1, $n2)}
function Invoke-MyDivide ($n1, $n2) {$MyMath.MyDivide($n1, $n2)}
function Invoke-MyTest () {$MyMath.MyTest()}
```

This example is for illustration purposes. With some additional thought and work, though, we can make it generic by parameterizing the final snippet. We can:

- Add a $Type parameter, which lets us pass in any type for inspection
- Add a Where filter parameter, to be used when the methods are piped from GetMethods
- Add a variable name parameter, so we don't have to hardcode $MyMath

One final thought: the text manipulation tools that PowerShell brings to the table are invaluable for doing many types of transforms. In the next sections, you'll see a few more. These ideas are not new. PowerShell's deep integration into Windows and the .NET Framework are what makes it possible for developers to optimize their efforts.

Calling PowerShell Functions from C#

Next, we'll compile more C# and then create a custom object rather than a PSModuleInfo object using New-Module and the –AsCustomObject property. We'll create a single PowerShell function called test and store it in the variable $module so we can pass it to the constructor in the C# class. Finally, we'll call the C# InvokeTestMethod. InvokeTestMethod looks up the PowerShell test function in the module that was passed in the constructor. If the function is found, Invoke is called, all the ducks line up, and PowerShell prints "Hello World".

This next example using `Add-Type` will work if you're using PowerShell v3.

If you are using PowerShell v2 and have not added *powershell.exe.config* to point to .NET 4.0, see Appendix A.

If you're not sure what version of the .NET runtime your session is using, type `$PSVersionTable` and look for the `CLRVersion` entry.

```
Add-Type @"
using System.Management.Automation;

public class InvokePSModuleMethod
{
    PSObject module;
    public InvokePSModuleMethod(PSObject module)
    {
        this.module = module;
    }

    public void InvokeTestMethod()
    {
        var method = module.Methods["test"];

        if(method != null) method.Invoke();
    }
}
"@

$module = New-Module -AsCustomObject {
    function test { "Hello World" | Out-Host }
}

(New-Object InvokePSModuleMethod $module).InvokeTestMethod()
```

That's a long trek to get Hello World printed; we could have just typed `"Hello World"` at the command line, after all. But there's a method to the madness.

In the next section, we will use these pieces to create a visitor that uses PowerShell v3's new access to the *abstract syntax tree* (AST). We will read PowerShell source code and extract information by parsing it, not just scanning for text patterns.

A hat tip goes to Jason Shirk, one of the PowerShell team's language experts, who shared the technique.

Overriding C# Methods with PowerShell Functions

OK, I've shown you how to pull out the metadata from compiled C# code and generate PowerShell functions to wrap it. This is extremely useful when you're exploring a new .NET DLL. We can quickly extract key information about the component and start kicking the tires right from the command line. Plus, because the .NET component is wrapped in PowerShell functions, we can seamlessly plug into the PowerShell ecosystem, further optimizing our time and effort. For example, if the component returns arrays of objects, we can use the `Where`, `Group`, and `Measure` cmdlets to filter and summarize information rapidly.

Now we'll move on to overriding C# base class methods with PowerShell functions.

The next example extracts metadata from a .NET DLL, generates C# methods overriding the base class methods, and creates a constructor that takes a PowerShell module.

Each of the C# methods doing the override uses the technique in the previous section to look up the method in the PowerShell module and call it with the correct parameters.

I'm using the AST capabilities of PowerShell v3 to demonstrate the technique of extracting method signatures from C# and then injecting a PowerShell module to override the implementation. This is valid for PowerShell v2 and can be applied to .NET solutions employing inheritance.

The Breakdown

I'm going to break this script down into a few sections: the metadata extraction of the PowerShell v3 `AstVisitor` methods, the subsequent C# code generation that puts the PowerShell "hooks" in place, and the creation of the PowerShell custom object using `New-Module`. This example will have a PowerShell function called `VisitFunction` and mirrors the method I override in the base class `AstVisitor`. This PowerShell function will be called each time a function is found in our source script. `VisitFunction` takes `$ast` as a parameter and contains all the information about the function that has been matched in our source script. I'll be pulling out only the name and line number where it was matched.

Looking for PowerShell Functions

In this source script, we want to find where all the functions are defined.

```
function test1 {"Say Hello"}
1..10 | % {$_}
function test2 {"Say Goodbye"}
1..10 | % {$_}
function test3 {"Another function"}
#function test4 {"This is a comment"}
```

We can see three functions named test1, test2, test3, and they are on lines 1, 3, and 5. The last function, test4, is a comment. I included it for two reasons. First, if we were scanning the file using `Select-String` and pattern matching on function, this would show up in the results and be misleading. Second, with the AST approach, test4 will be recognized as a comment and therefore not included in the results of our search for functions.

While it is easy to scan a file visually, if I'm looking at a large script with many functions, I'd like an automated way to know what and where my functions are. Plus, if I can extract this information programmatically, the potential is there to automate many other activities.

Extracting Metadata and Generating C#

Here we'll generate something a little more complex, leveraging the Invoke-Template we built before. The goal is to create a C# class that has all of the override methods found in System.Management.Automation.Language.AstVisitor. This is equivalent to being in Visual Studio, inheriting from AstVisitor, overriding each method, and then providing an implementation.

```
public override AstVisitAction $FunctionName($ParameterName ast)
{
    var method = module.Methods["$FunctionName"];
    if (method != null)
    {
        method.Invoke(ast);
    }
    return AstVisitAction.Continue;
}
```

The implementation we want to provide, for each overridden method, is a lookup for that function name in the module/custom object passed from PowerShell. If one is found, we'll invoke it and pass it the AST for the declaration being visited.

```
[System.Management.Automation.Language.AstVisitor].GetMethods() |
    Where { $_.Name -like 'Visit*' } |
    ForEach {
        $functionName = $_.Name
        $parameterName = $_.GetParameters()[0].ParameterType.Name

        Get-Template AstVisitAction.txt
    }
```

This is the template that gets it done; the file is named *AstVisitAction.txt*.

Now we move on to the PowerShell code snippet that'll figure out the FunctionName and ParameterName and invoke the template that does the code generation.

The GetMethods() method returns a list of methods on the Type System.Management.Automation.Language.AstVisitor. We're filtering the list of methods to only the ones whose names begin with Visit*—that is, Where { $_.Name -like 'Visit*' }. In the ForEach, we grab the name of the function $_.Name and the name of the parameter type being passed to it, $_.GetParameters()[0].ParameterType.Name.

```
using System;
using System.Management.Automation;
```

```
using System.Management.Automation.Language;

public class CommandMatcher : AstVisitor
{
    PSObject module;
    public CommandMatcher(PSObject module)
    {
        this.module = module;
    }

    $methodOverrides
}
```

The template sets up references, a constructor, and a backing store for the module being passed in. The key piece is the $methodOverrides variable. This will contain all the text generated from the previous template, *AstVisitAction.txt*.

```
. .\Invoke-Template.ps1
Invoke-Template $pwd\etc {

    $methodOverrides = Invoke-Template $pwd\etc {
      [System.Management.Automation.Language.AstVisitor].GetMethods() |
        Where { $_.Name -like 'Visit*' } |
        ForEach {
            $functionName = $_.Name
            $parameterName = $_.GetParameters()[0].ParameterType.Name

            Get-Template AstVisitAction.txt
        }
    }

    Get-Template CommandMatcher.txt
}
```

This is the completed script that generates a C# class ready for compilation. This class handles visiting any PowerShell source, calling out to a PowerShell function to handle the node that is visited. We'll go over that next.

Fortunately, it's not necessary to understand the recursive descent parser mechanism. The fundamental point here is the metadata extraction and code generation, which is the glide path to using the Add-Type cmdlet and compiling useful code on the fly in the current context.

The PowerShell Module

Now that we have code-generated all of the overrides for the base class AstVisitor, we will create a PowerShell module to pass to it that will be called back every time a PowerShell function definition is detected.

```
$m = New-Module -AsCustomObject {

    $script:FunctionList = @()
```

```
    function VisitFunctionDefinition ($ast) {
        $script:FunctionList += New-Object PSObject -Property @{
            Kind = "Function"
            Name = $ast.Name
            StartLineNumber = $ast.Extent.StartLineNumber
        }
    }

    function GetFunctionList {$script:FunctionList}
}
```

We store this in the variable $m, and will pass it to the constructor later.

I added a helper function, GetFunctionList, which returns the script scoped variable. FunctionList is initialized to an empty array to start and is populated in VisitFunction Definition.

Each time a function declaration is matched, the PowerShell function VisitFunction Definition is invoked. We then emit a PowerShell object with three parameters, Kind, Name, and StartLineNumber. We hardcode Kind, for simplicity, and get the other two values from the data passed in the $ast variable.

Testing It All

We'll now create a reusable helper function that takes a PowerShell script and returns the AST that can be "visited"; let's call it Get-Ast. Next, we'll "new" up the Command Matcher we built in C# during the code-generation phase and pass in $m, which contains our PowerShell module with the function we want to invoke. The variable $ast contains the AST of the script passed in the here-string. The variable $ast is a System.Manage ment.Automation.Language.ScriptBlockAst, and the method we want to invoke is Visit(). We will pass $matcher, our custom visitor, to it. Finally, we will call $m.Get FunctionList(), displaying the details about the functions that were found.

```
function Get-Ast
{
    param([string]$script)

    [System.Management.Automation.Language.Parser]::ParseInput(
        $script,
        [ref]$null,
        [ref]$null
    )
}

$matcher = New-Object CommandMatcher $m

$ast = Get-Ast @'
function test {"Say Hello"}
1..10 | % {$_}
function test1 {"Say Goodbye"}
1..10 | % {$_}
function test2 {"Another function"}
```

```
'@

$ast.Visit($matcher)
$m.GetFunctionList()
```

This correctly finds the three functions in our test script, displaying the name of the function and the line it is on as follows:

```
Name   StartLineNumber Kind
----   --------------- ----
test                 1 Function
test1                3 Function
test2                5 Function
```

You can easily rework this to process a single script or an entire directory of scripts. In addition, you can add a filename as a property, thus enabling filtering of function names and filenames. This way, we can semantically scan any number of PowerShell scripts for a particular function name and quickly locate the file and line number where it lives.

We can also add more functions to the PowerShell module to match on parameters, variable expressions, and more. From there, we could create a new `PSObject` with the properties we wanted and then we'd have a list of key information about our scripts that we could programmatically act on.

Using PowerShell's `System.Management.Automation.Language` library like this is only one application of what the library can do. There is a lot to explore here that is beyond the scope of this book. If you're familiar with the tool ReSharper from JetBrains and its ability to refactor C# code, you'll have an idea of the potential of `System.Manage ment.Automation.Language`. For example, you could use it to rename part of a PowerShell function name and ripple that change through an entire script accurately. Another example is extracting a section of PowerShell code as a function, naming it, adding it to the script, and replacing where it came from with the new function name. Doing static analysis along the lines of the lint tool PSLint (*http://bit.ly/bI9sLz*)? No problem with `System.Management.Automation.Language`.

This doesn't come for free. You need to learn the ins and outs of this library. There is much potential here for some great open source tools for PowerShell as well as opportunities to learn more about what this platform offers.

Summary

In this chapter, I showed several ways to use PowerShell to work with information, transform it, and position it for consumption elsewhere. The information was stored in C# files and text files, and it was even extracted directly from compiled DLLs. These ideas can also be extended to SQL Server schemas, XML, JSON, and even Microsoft Excel. Because it's based on .NET, PowerShell easily integrates with all of these tools.

As a developer, I reuse and expand these approaches for every project I work on. I actively seek out patterns in the workflow and automate them. This has numerous benefits. Code generation has been around as long as software languages. PowerShell's deep integration to the .NET platform and its game-changing object pipeline optimizes the development effort. Being able to crack open a DLL and inspect methods and parameters—all from within a subexpression in a here-string—and then compile it on the fly in a single page of code enables developers to iterate through ideas more rapidly.

Finally, being able to extend C# solutions by invoking PowerShell—and here is the key—*without having to touch the original C# code*, is huge. As you might know, scripting languages are sometimes referred to as glue languages or system integration languages. PowerShell, being based on .NET, takes this definition to a whole new level.

## CHAPTER 5

Add PowerShell to Your GUI

Adding scripting support to your application is one of the most valuable things you can do for your client, letting them add value to your software, and keep it current over time with little or no overhead from the developers.

—Roy Osherove, author and consultant
(*http://bit.ly/K0xClG*)

When you add PowerShell to an application, other developers, end users, testers, and system integrators can customize the application's logic to better match their specific needs. This approach is an efficient use of resources; developers can focus their efforts on core functionality while allowing others to easily and independently customize the application as they desire. Using PowerShell in this way obviates the need to distribute the application source code for other developers to extend the application. As a result, you do not need to support multiple versions of the application.

Thus, not only does adding PowerShell to an application speed software development, but it also allows for common areas of application customization such as modifying code to match particular businesses processes, automating repetitive tasks, adding unique features, and accessing internal and remote data.

Embedding PowerShell in your C# Application

PowerShell is surfaced as a command-line application (the console), a scripting language, and an API. In this section, I'll show you the API and how simple it is to create the PowerShell engine, call some cmdlets, and print out the results.

 You'll need to add a reference to PowerShell to follow along with these examples. To do so, open the project file as a text file and add the following line into the `<ItemGroup>` section:

```
<Reference Include="System.Management.Automation" />
```

I've set up two C# extension methods, `ExecutePS()` and `WritePS()`. `ExecutePS()` extends strings, and `WritePS()` extends `List<PSObject>`. The strings are the PowerShell commands, and the `List<PSObject>` is the result of invoking those commands.

By default, the `ExecutePS()` method prints the results to the console. If you pass false to `ExecutePS()`, it returns a list of `PSObjects`. PowerShell v3 takes a dependency on the *dynamic language runtime* (DLR; *http://bit.ly/9EzVgF*), and `PSObject` implements `IDynamicObject`. This lets us do a `ForEach` over the results and take advantage of late binding to get at the `ProcessName`.

 The `ForEach` block requires PowerShell v3 to be installed. If you only have PowerShell v2, comment out the `ForEach` block, and the example will run cleanly.

```
using System;
using System.Collections.Generic;
using System.Linq;
using System.Management.Automation;

class Program
{
    private static void Main()
    {
        var script = "Get-Process | Where {$_.Handles -gt 400}";

        // Let the extension method
        // print out the results
        script.ExecutePS();

        // In PowerShell v3, PSObject
        // implements IDynamicObject
        foreach (dynamic item in
            script.ExecutePS(writeToConsole: false))
        {
            Console.WriteLine(item.ProcessName);
        }
    }
}

public static class PSExtensions
{
    public static List<PSObject> ExecutePS(
        this string script, bool writeToConsole = true)
    {
        var powerShell = PowerShell
                .Create()
                .AddScript(script);

        if (writeToConsole)
        {
            powerShell.AddCommand("Out-String");
```

```
            powerShell
                .Invoke<PSObject>()
                .ToList()
                .WritePS();
        }

        // Lets the caller act on the returned collection
        // of PowerShell objects
        return powerShell
            .Invoke<PSObject>()
            .ToList();
    }

    public static void WritePS(this List<PSObject> psResults)
    {
        psResults.ForEach(i => Console.WriteLine(i));
    }
}
```

The `script` variable contains the PowerShell commands. The `ExecutePS()` method creates the PowerShell engine and then adds the commands with the `AddScript()` method. We use the `AddCommand()` method to append the `Out-String` cmdlet to whatever is specified in the `script` variable. This tells PowerShell to convert the objects returned to their string representations. PowerShell will execute all of this after we call the `Invoke()` method.

The `Invoke()` method returns an array of PowerShell `PSObjects`. Just as `System.Object` is the root of the type system in .NET, `PSObject` is the root of the synthetic type system in PowerShell.

The `WritePS()` method extends `List<PSObject>` by looping through the results and printing it to the console.

This example shows how easy it is to include the PowerShell engine in your application. You can use all of the PowerShell cmdlets with this approach, including external scripts and modules developed by you, others in the community, third parties, or Microsoft.

I do not include any error management, profile loading, or REPL consoles here. If you want to see such functionality in action, plus learn how to load your application objects into the PowerShell run space, read on to see what you can do with the Beaver Music application.

The Beaver Music application is a Windows Presentation Foundation (WPF) GUI application, and I layer a simple WPF PowerShell console into it. It is a command line in my WPF GUI, capable of working with all the objects in my app, including the Managed Extensibility Framework (MEF) container and more. The best news is, it's included with the book and can be easily hooked into any of your GUI apps too. Let's get started.

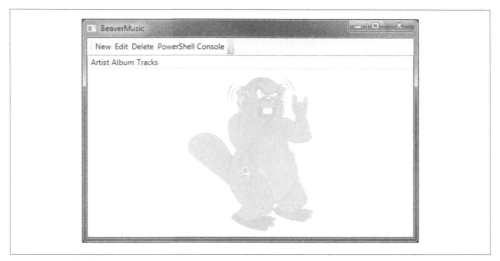

Figure 5-1. The Beaver Music app

WPF is a computer-software graphical subsystem for rendering user interfaces in Windows-based applications.

Beaver Music Application

The reference application for this chapter, Beaver Music, is a very simple music album management system. It supports create, read, update, and delete (CRUD) actions for albums. Beaver Music has the functionality you'd expect—a couple of dialogs for adding and changing album information, and you can delete albums as well. What we want to focus on is the PowerShell Console button (shown in Figure 5-1), a WPF application that has the PowerShell engine embedded in it. As noted earlier, PowerShell is surfaced as a console, a scripting language, and an API; the custom PowerShell console uses this surfaced API in conjunction with the Beaver Music application so it can be scripted and automated. This works similarly to the way Microsoft Excel can be automated with the embedded Visual Basic for Applications (VBA) scripting language.

PowerShell Console

After clicking on the PowerShell Console button, you'll see Figure 5-2.

Each time the console is launched, I inject variables, which are instances of the running components. For example, the top pane is a WPF textbox. I added a textbox reference into the PowerShell run space, setting it to the variable name $ScriptPane. If I want to change the background color of the $ScriptPane, I can type $ScriptPane.Background = "Cyan" and press F5, and the background color of the textbox will change at runtime.

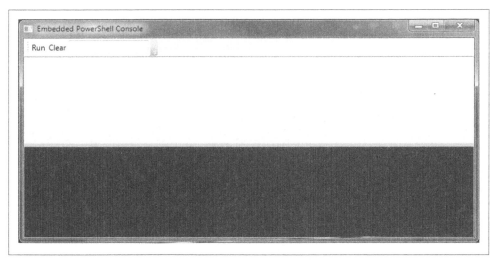

Figure 5-2. PowerShell Console button

The top pane is where you type in PowerShell commands or scripts; to execute them, either click Run or press F5. The bottom pane will show the results. It's a full-fledged PowerShell engine, so you can type any valid PowerShell (actually, you can even type invalid PowerShell, and you'll see the errors in the bottom pane). The Beaver Music PowerShell Console is custom and does not have all the niceties found in the Microsoft PowerShell console or in the Integrated Scripting Environment (ISE).

The source to this application is available at *https://github.com/dfinke/powershell-for developers*, so feel free to enhance it or build your own. If you do, be sure to post it to a social coding platform like GitHub so others can use it, change it, and benefit from it, too.

What makes the Beaver Music Console custom? You should be able to embed it in any WPF application. The console is a WPF component layered on top of a PowerShell engine. Plus, it supports a profile; to access it, type **notepad $profile** and press F5. You can store PowerShell functions here, and they will be available each time you run the application. Also, custom variables will be added through both the profile and the C# code that are not available in other PowerShell consoles like the command line and PowerShell ISE.

I've also injected live instances of the main Beaver Music application. For example, the WPF application has an album repository. The repository is the in-memory data store for holding all the albums. I've added it using the `AddVariable()` method.

```
PSConfig.AddVariable("AlbumRepository", _albumRepository);
```

This means we can get to the live instance of `_albumRepository` from the PowerShell variable `$AlbumRepository`. Since this is a PowerShell console, we can inspect the methods on that variable using `Get-Member` (see Figure 5-3).

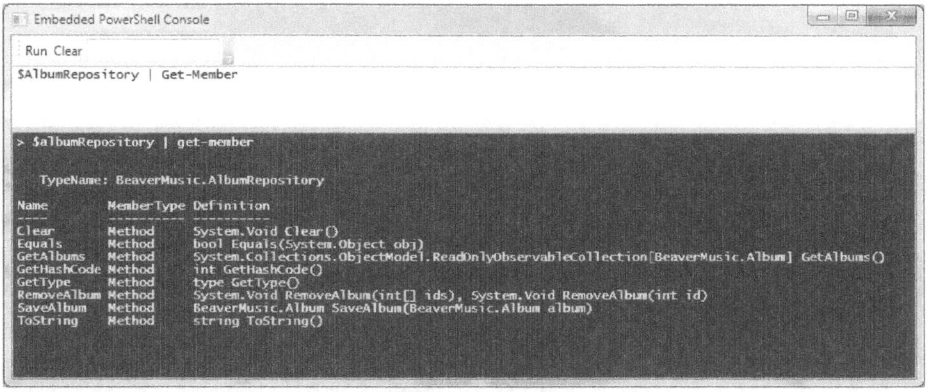

Figure 5-3. Inspecting the methods on AlbumRepository

Foundational Functions

The live objects of the Beaver Music application are added to the PowerShell engine, so now we can write PowerShell functions that take advantage of them. I've created five of them, and they follow the PowerShell naming standards of *Verb-Noun*. You can find the PowerShell-approved verbs by typing Get-Verb at the command prompt. The ones I've created are Add-Album, Clear-Album, Get-Album, New-Album, and Remove-Album. They support the CRD of the CRUD model nicely; I did not implement an update function in PowerShell.

I want to highlight that on three of the five functions I have decorated the parameters with either ValueFromPipelineByPropertyName or ValueFromPipeline. These two attributes really make PowerShell sing when you're piping objects between functions.

New-Album

Following is the New-Album function. We associate each of its parameters with Value FromPipelineByPropertyName, which indicates that the parameter can take values from a property of the incoming pipeline object that has the same name as the parameter.

```
function New-Album  {

    param(
        [Parameter(ValueFromPipelineByPropertyName=$true)]
        [string]$Name,
        [Parameter(ValueFromPipelineByPropertyName=$true)]
        [string]$Artist
    )

    Process {
        $album = New-Object BeaverMusic.Album
```

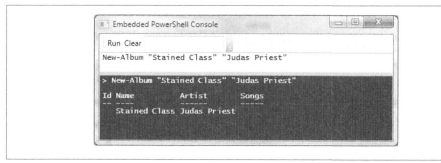

Figure 5-4. New-Album in action

```
        $album.Name   = $Name
        $album.Artist = $Artist

        $album
    }
}
```

New-Album takes two parameters, Name and Artist, and returns a BeaverMusic.Album object with those properties set (see Figure 5-4). The next example leverages the pipeline and the ValueFromPipelineByPropertyName.

Add-Album

Next is the Add-Album function. ValueFromPipeline indicates whether the parameter can take values from incoming pipeline objects. We need to specify a Process block, which indicates it will execute once for each $album that is passed from the pipeline. An added benefit is that we can also use traditional parameter passing.

```
function Add-Album {
    param(
        [Parameter(ValueFromPipeline=$true)]
        $album
    )

    Process {
        $AlbumRepository.SaveAlbum($album) | Out-Null
    }
}
```

This assumes $AlbumList contains an array of PowerShell objects that have been set up using the New-Album function. These objects will have two properties, Name and Artist.

```
ForEach($Album in $AlbumList) {
    Add-Album $Album
}
```

Next up, I'll show a different and far simpler syntax that fully leverages PowerShell's parameter binding mechanism, which is enabled with the `ValueFromPipeline` and `Process` block approach.

Import-Csv

We have *all* of PowerShell available to us and we don't want to build up our list of albums by hand. Instead, we'll store a list of them—or download one—in a CSV file.

```
Artist,Name
"Michael Jackson","Thriller"
"AC/DC","Back in Black"
"Pink Floyd","The Dark Side of the Moon"
"Whitney Houston / Various artists","The Bodyguard"
"Meat Loaf","Bat Out of Hell"
"Eagles","Their Greatest Hits"
"Various artists","Dirty Dancing"
"Backstreet Boys","Millennium"
"Bee Gees / Various artists","Saturday Night Fever"
"Fleetwood Mac","Rumours"
"Shania Twain","Come On Over"
"Led Zeppelin","Led Zeppelin IV"
"Alanis Morissette","Jagged Little Pill"
"The Beatles","Sgt. Pepper's Lonely Hearts Club Band"
"Celine Dion","Falling into You"
"Mariah Carey","Music Box"
"Michael Jackson","Dangerous"
"Celine Dion","Let's Talk About Love"
"Bee Gees","Spirits Having Flown"
"Bruce Springsteen","Born in the U.S.A."
"Dire Straits","Brothers in Arms"
"James Horner","Titanic"
"Madonna","The Immaculate Collection"
"Michael Jackson","Bad"
"Pink Floyd","The Wall"
"Nirvana","Nevermind"
```

We use the PowerShell cmdlet `Import-Csv` to read the file. This cmdlet creates an array of objects, each object having an **Artist** and **Name** property. These property names are determined from the first line of the file (see Figure 5-5).

Next, we'll pipe this to `New-Album`. Here is the parameter binding at work—remember, we set that up using `ValueFromPipeline` and the `Process` block. The `Import-Csv` is transformed into album objects with the correct properties set. Finally, we pipe the results to `Add-Album` so they are stored in the album repository and ultimately displayed in the Beaver Music main window (see Figure 5-6).

```
Import-Csv .\albums.csv | New-Album | Add-Album
```

Notice that we do not have to handle looping, end of files, or parameter passing. This is a very different approach to programming compared to C#, and I can't stress enough how much time and effort it saves. In fewer than 50 characters, we're exercising (testing) several code paths in our application. With a few more characters, we'll be clearing and

Figure 5-5. Import-Csv from albums.csv

filtering the list of albums and even pulling data from the Internet to create lists of albums.

Get-Album and Clear-Album

I wrapped the previous 50 characters in a function and called it Import-Default (Figure 5-7). I'm now exercising a chunk of my app with 15 characters. I type that in and add Get-Album, which reads all the albums currently in the repository (Figure 5-8).

Managing Applications Better with PowerShell

Now we're interacting with live data in a live environment in our application. If we run this script again, pressing F5, we will have duplicate records. To we'll add the Clear-Album at the top in order to work with an empty repository each time.

Let's use some more built-in PowerShell. We know there are 26 songs in our CSV file, but we need to make sure that after pushing all that data through the multiple code paths, we do in fact end up with that number of albums in the repository (Figure 5-9).

Figure 5-6. Importing and adding albums to the repository

So, we clear the repository, import the defaults, retrieve all the albums, and count them with the PowerShell cmdlet `Measure` (which is an alias to `Measure-Object`), and sure enough, we get the correct count.

One more tweak, and it reads like a unit test (Figure 5-10).

Importing Albums from the Web

Information is stored in many formats as well as many locations. When I am testing the Beaver Music application, I like to flow lots of different data through it. This exercises different aspects of the applications and lets me figure out how to handle data that I may not expect. Often it's the case that the Web has ready-made data sources I can tap into. I might need to scrub the data a bit, deleting unwanted details, combining others, and then emitting PowerShell objects with properties so I can let it play into the

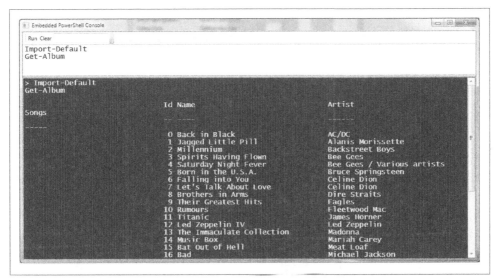

Figure 5-7. These commands update the GUI and the results pane

pipeline. In this example, I took *albums.csv* and made it available from my website. We'll create a new function, `Get-AlbumFromWeb`, and then pipe it just the way we did before, first to `New-Album` and then to `Add-Album`, and—bingo!—we get the same number of albums. This time, I reached out over the Internet, got my data, and displayed it all from within the same PowerShell console (Figure 5-11).

Function Get-AlbumFromWeb

Interacting with the Web is not native in PowerShell v2 (though it is in v3), so we reach into the .NET Framework, create a new `Net.WebClient`, and use the `DownloadString()` method.

```
function Get-AlbumFromWeb {
    $wc=New-Object Net.WebClient
    $url="http://dougfinke.com/PowerShellForDevelopers/albums.csv"

    $wc.DownloadString($url) |
      ConvertFrom-Csv
}
```

We're pulling down the contents of a CSV file so we can pipe it to `ConvertFrom-Csv` (another built-in PowerShell cmdlet), and now the data is ready to be piped to our functions that load it into the music repository.

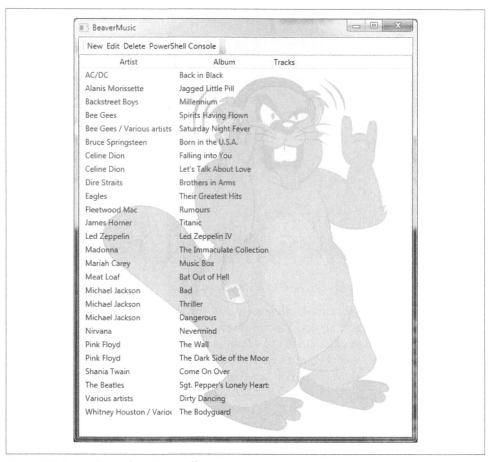

Figure 5-8. Importing and retrieving albums

PowerShell v3

I've got PowerShell v3 CTP2 installed, so I can replace my function `Get-AlbumFromWeb` with this new one in v3, `Invoke-RestMethod`, to get the same result with fewer lines of code (Figure 5-12).

Out-GridView

`Out-GridView`, mentioned previously in Chapter 3 and Chapter 4 and shown in Figure 5-13, is a great tool that debuted in PowerShell v2.

```
Import-Default
Get-Album | Out-GridView
```

Figure 5-9. Counting the albums

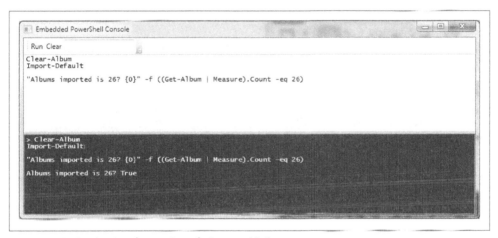

Figure 5-10. Confirming the number of albums added

Bottom line, it is a separate interactive window that supports filtering and sorting. In PowerShell v3, you can use the `-PassThru` parameter to select items and have them passed through to the pipeline. I use it in the custom PowerShell Console to great effect.

Export-ToExcel

Getting data into Excel is extremely helpful for analysis, not to mention it gives us access to PivotTables, charting, and more. PowerShell doesn't have anything out the box for working with Excel, but not to worry. Transforming data is another sweet spot for PowerShell.

```
function Export-ToExcel {
    param(
```

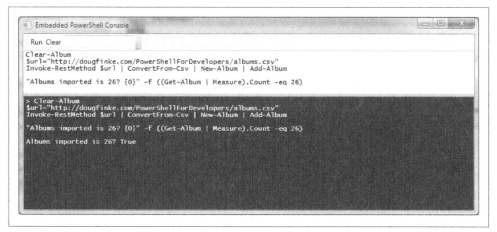

Figure 5-11. Importing the albums from a website

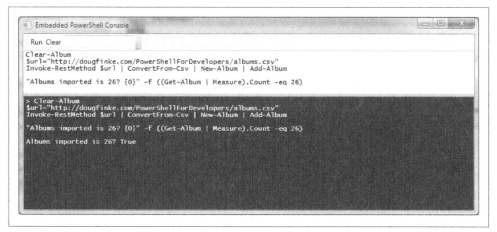

Figure 5-12. PowerShell v3 Invoke-RestMethod

```
        $fileName = "$pwd\BeaverMusic.csv"
    )

    Get-Album |
      Export-Csv -NoTypeInformation $fileName

    Invoke-Item $fileName
}
```

The Export-ToExcel function uses one of the foundation functions, Get-Album, to get all the albums in the repository. It then pipes that data to Export-Csv, another built-in PowerShell cmdlet. Export-Csv takes an array of objects and saves it to a CSV file. It gets the names for the data columns from the names of the properties on the object. In the last line of the script, we call Invoke-Item (yet another built-in PowerShell cmdlet),

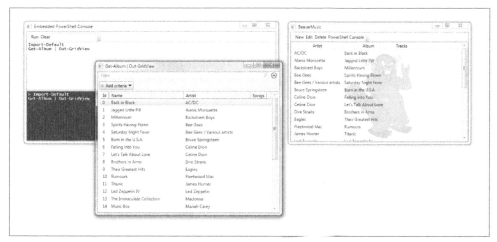

Figure 5-13. Dumping live data to Out-GridView

Figure 5-14. Dumping live data to Excel

passing it the filename used in the export. `Invoke-Item` performs the default action on the specified item; in this case, the default action associated with CSV files opens it in Excel, as shown in Figure 5-14.

Here is all you need to make that happen:

```
Import-Default
Export-ToExcel
```

I regularly use the `Export-Csv`/`Invoke-Item` technique in both the console and ISE. I find it an invaluable way to work with data.

Interacting with MEF

MEF is Microsoft's Managed Extensibility Framework; it's a composition layer for .NET that improves the flexibility, maintainability, and testability of applications. The principle purpose of MEF is *extensibility*—that is, to serve as a "plug-in" framework in situations when the application developer and the plug-in developer differ and have no particular knowledge of each other beyond a published interface library.

Another problem space MEF addresses, and one of its major strengths, is *discovery*. MEF has a lot of, well, extensible discovery mechanisms that operate on metadata you can associate with extensions.

```
$MEFHelper.GetMEFCatalog.Parts | Select DisplayName
$Contract = "BeaverMusic.UI.Shell.AlbumListViewModel"
$MEFHelper.GetExport($Contract).NewAlbumCommand.Execute($null)
```

In the preceding example, I've injected a C# instance of `MEFHelper` and tied it to the PowerShell variable `MEFHelper`. `MEFHelper` is a C# instance that has a few methods—for example, the `GetExport()` method takes a `contractName` and carries this implementation:

```
return ExportProvider.GetExport<object>(contractName).Value;
```

Using this and the other methods, we can discover which MEF parts are in the catalog, then retrieve a live instance from the MEF catalog and act on it. In this case, we're looking for the Album List View Model; from there, we can get at the command that launches the new album dialog window (Figure 5-15).

MEF helps provide an extensive, automatable infrastructure for an application. In addition, being mindful of the development of the static components will enable them to seamlessly work in PowerShell. Developing your .NET components with an eye toward PowerShell integration will actually help you create a better-designed infrastructure.

Discovering the executable commands

So, again, we want to find all of the commands we can execute on the `AlbumListView Model`. Using a combination of the `$MEFHelper` and PowerShell's `Get-Member`, we can find all the properties whose names end in "Command" using the wildcard `*Command`. (This is how I found the `NewAlbumCommand` in the previous example in the live running application. Calling the `Execute()` method then brought up the dialog window, where I could enter album details.)

```
$MEFHelper.GetExport('BeaverMusic.UI.Shell.AlbumListViewModel') |
    Get-Member -MemberType Property -Name *Command

    TypeName: BeaverMusic.UI.Shell.AlbumListViewModel

Name                    MemberType
----                    ----------
```

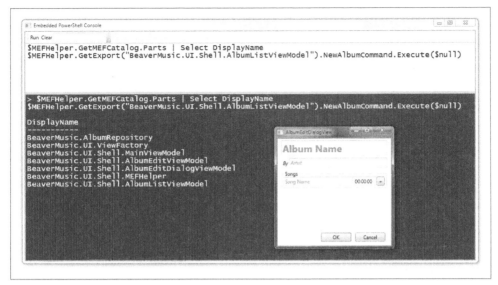

Figure 5-15. Returning MEF catalog parts

DeleteAlbumCommand	Property
EditAlbumCommand	Property
NewAlbumCommand	Property
PowerShellConsoleCommand	Property

The discovery and application doesn't end here. We could go further and call methods and properties on the dialog to set default information; wrapping that in a PowerShell function is in essence creating a macro for that part of the system. Providing this for end users can really open up productivity.

Show-NewAlbumDialog

Working with MEF and .NET APIs can be verbose. I'll create a higher level abstraction for the previous snippet so it is simpler to use and easier to compose. Plus, this is a step towards creating a "vocabulary" for the application (Figure 5-16).

```
function Show-NewAlbumDialog {
    $contractName = "BeaverMusic.UI.Shell.AlbumListViewModel"
    $MEFHelper.GetExport($contractName).NewAlbumCommand.Execute($null)
}
```

Implementing Performance Counters

We've only scratched the surface of PowerShell's reach. In this example, we'll tap into the Windows performance counters using Get-PrivateBytes, which wraps Get-Counter (a built-in PowerShell cmdlet), showing the amount of memory the application is using before and after we retrieve music information from Yahoo! using YQL in the query.

Figure 5-16. Using Show-NewAlbumDialog

```
"Private Bytes before loading albums from Yahoo $(Get-PrivateBytes)"

Clear-Album
Get-YahooMusic | New-Album | Add-Album

"Private Bytes after loading albums from Yahoo $(Get-PrivateBytes)"
```

Here is the result:

```
Get-YahooMusic | New-Album | Add-Album

"Private Bytes after loading albums from Yahoo $(Get-PrivateBytes)"
Private Bytes before loading albums from Yahoo 93548544
Private Bytes after loading albums from Yahoo 95088640
```

It's not a far leap from here to exercising code paths in your application and gathering metrics about memory, CPU, disk activity, and more.

I've added the code for Get-PrivateBytes and Get-YahooMusic for reading convenience.

Get-PrivateBytes

```
function Get-PrivateBytes {
    $counterName="\Process($(Get-CurrentProcessName))\Private Bytes"
    (Get-Counter $counterName).CounterSamples |
        Select -Expand CookedValue
}
```

Get-Counter comes with PowerShell and can retrieve performance counter data, the same that you'd see in PerfMon. Here we grab the CounterSamples property and then expand the `CookedValue` property. This is an extremely useful way to execute different code paths of your application and then measure your performance counter data.

Get-YahooMusic

`Get-YahooMusic` uses the `WebClient` in the .NET Framework, so we can download a string via the Yahoo API using the Yahoo Query Language (YQL) to query music data. Data is returned as XML—no problem for PowerShell—and we can transform that result into an array of objects with the correct properties, `Artist` and `Name`, then pipe it directly into the application.

```
function Get-YahooMusic {
    $wc = New-Object Net.WebClient
    $url = "http://query.yahooapis.com/v1/public/yql?q=select * from
music.release.popular"
    [xml]$xml = $wc.DownloadString($url)

    $xml.query.results.Release |
        ForEach {
            New-Object PSObject -Property @{
                Artist=$_.artist.name
                Name=$_.Title
            }
        }
}
```

Once you get going with this powerful approach, you'll be amazed by the reach you have for data acquisition. No C# needed!

```
Get-YahooMusic | New Album | Add-Album
```

Figure 5-17 shows the results.

From here, we can go wild with the Yahoo! interface. We can easily add parameters to the function to be passed to the YQL to subset the data. We can also quickly set up other functions that use different YQL to retrieve other types of music details.

Wiring a Textbox to Execute PowerShell Code

In the next example, I've included the Chinook sample XML music file along with two PowerShell functions, `Get-ChinookData` and `Import-BeaverMusic`. You can find the Chinook database on CodePlex (*http://bit.ly/YPbVd*). Run `Get-ChinookData`, and it will pull the information from the XML file and display it as albums in the console. You can also filter the data by artist name. The filtering uses a match, so you don't need to be exact. Piping this to the `Import-BeaverMusic` function will clear the albums in the main window list view and add the new albums, as shown in Figure 5-18.

The function `Get-ChinookData` uses the PowerShell XML accelerator to create an `XmlDo cument` from the contents of the file *ChinookData.xml*. Rather than using the built-in `Get-Content` cmdlet, I use the `ReadAllLines()` method on the `IO.File` namespace. This is a faster way to read a file.

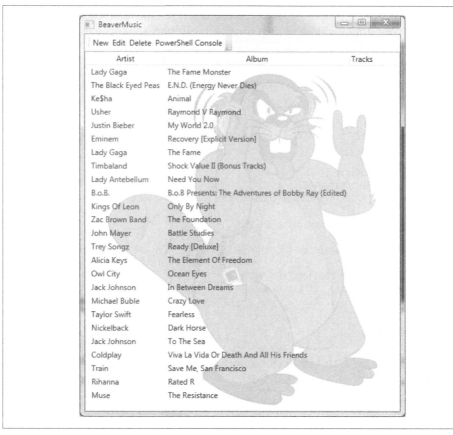

Figure 5-17. Get-YahooMusic results

Also, I cache the data by checking for the global variable $global:ChinookData. In the last line of the script, I filter the data by artist using the Where cmdlet. Note, if $artist is not specified, all of the data is returned.

```
function Get-ChinookData ($artist) {
    if(!$global:ChinookData) {
        [xml]$global:ChinookData =
            [IO.File]::ReadAllLines("$pwd\ChinookData.xml")
    }

    if(!$global:artists) {

        $global:artists = @{}
        $global:ChinookData.ChinookDataSet.Artist |
            ForEach {
                $artists.($_.ArtistId)= $_.Name
            }
    }

    $(ForEach($item in $global:ChinookData.ChinookDataSet.Album) {
```

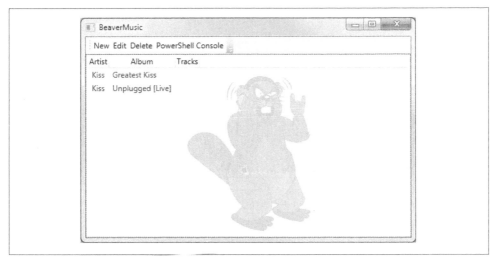

Figure 5-18. Using Get-ChinookData to import albums

```
        New-Album $item.Title $artists.($item.ArtistId)
    }) | Where {$_.Artist -match $artist}
}
```

Here we're looking for any artist with the word "Kiss" in it.

```
Get-ChinookData Kiss | Import-BeaverMusic
```

Working in the PreviewKeyDown

Once we've written PowerShell scripts and tested them like this, it'd be a shame if we could use them only at the console. We could really reduce the test matrix by not having to reimplement reading the XML and adding the albums to the repository in C# code. Plus, we could save a lot of time reusing those PowerShell functions directly in the application.

```
private void Artist_PreviewKeyDown(
    object sender, System.Windows.Input.KeyEventArgs e)
{
    if (e.Key == Key.Enter)
    {
        var script = "Get-ChinookData "
            + Artist.Text + " | Import-BeaverMusic";

        script.ExecutePS();
        e.Handled = true;
    }
}
```

This is a bit of C# code that reacts to keystrokes in the textbox that sits in the PowerShell console. When the Enter key is pressed, we construct a PowerShell command as a string.

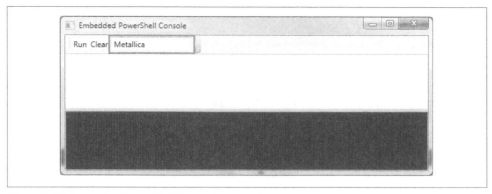

Figure 5-19. Executing PowerShell from a WPF textbox

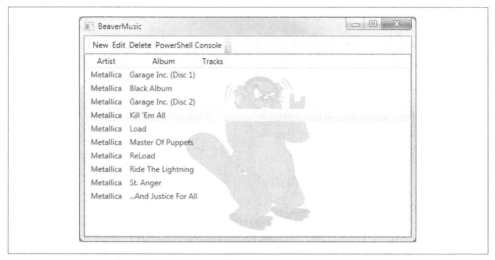

Figure 5-20. Results of executing PowerShell from a WPF textbox

```
var script = "Get-ChinookData "
           + Artist.Text + " | Import-BeaverMusic";
```

After we enter "Metallica" (see Figure 5-19) and press Enter, the `script` variable looks like this:

```
"Get-ChinookData Metallica | Import-BeaverMusic"
```

This line of C# code calls the extension method `ExecutePS()`. The returned results look as if we had typed it all in the PowerShell console, and the main window is updated with the results (see Figure 5-20).

```
script.ExecutePS();
```

Figure 5-21. Debugging in the Beaver Music app

This is a fantastic and simple way to expose PowerShell functionality in your .NET application. There is so much more that you can do here, so I'll leave it to you for now to experiment further.

Running Script and Debugging the C#

Here's a neat trick. Open *BeaverMusic.sln*, navigate to the BeaverMusic Project, and edit the *AlbumRepository.cs* file. Set a breakpoint in the GetAlbums() method. Run the application, launch the PowerShell console, type **Get-Album** in the script pane, and press F5.

You'll hit the break after running the script and land in the live running application. You'll be able to step through the C# code, inspect variables, and view the call stack just as you would expect. Too cool!

This is very powerful. You can create scripts that quickly put the application into a reproducible state and then debug it. When bugs are reported, you could potentially email PowerShell scripts around that reproduce the bugs—which is much more reliable than reading bug reports. See Figure 5-21 to view debugging in action.

Getting the PowerShell Console in Your App

Loading the PowerShell console in your application is pretty easy. First, download the code from Github (*http://bit.ly/KTZxEG*). You can add this method to your app. Then, either remove or customize the PSConfig.Profile and PSConfig.AddVariable statements.

```
    PSConsole _console;
    public void LaunchPowerShellConsole()
    {
        PSConfig.AddVariable("AlbumRepository", _albumRepository);
        PSConfig.Profile = "BeaverMusicProfile.ps1";

        _console = new PSConsole();
        _console.Closing +=
        new System.ComponentModel.CancelEventHandler(
          (w, e) => _console = null
        );

        _console.Show();
    }
```

PSConfig.Profile

Use the `PSConfig.Profile` statement to define the name of the PowerShell script that
will be stored in `$profile`. The console checks if this file exists and evaluates the script
content in the context of the session.

PSConfig.AddVariable

Use the `PSConfig.AddVariable` statement to inject the object model of your application
into the PowerShell session.

```
    PSConfig.AddVariable("AlbumRepository", _albumRepository);
```

Here, I use `_albumRepository`, which is the instantiated object, and I am tying it to the
PowerShell variable name `$AlbumRepository`. In the launched console, I can access it
with `$AlbumRepository`. Earlier in this chapter (Figure 5-3), I showed how you can
inspect the methods of this object at runtime. You can inject any kind and any number
of variables into the PowerShell session using the `AddVariable()` method. In addition,
you can name them whatever you'd like, and once inside the PowerShell console you
can access them by prefixing the name with a `$`.

The PowerShell Console Code

I'm not going to do a narrative on the code that supports the PowerShell console and
its configuration. It's about 125 lines, a couple of pages of code. I include it here only
as a reference.

PS.cs

```
    namespace EmbeddedPSConsole
    {
        public static class PS
        {
            public static string ExecutePS(this string script)
            {
```

```csharp
                var sb = new
                    StringBuilder(string.Format("> {0}\r", script));

                powerShell.AddScript(script);
                powerShell.AddCommand("Out-String");
                powerShell.AddParameter("Width", 133);

                try
                {
                    var results = powerShell.Invoke();
                    if (powerShell.Streams.Error.Count > 0)
                    {
                        foreach (var err in powerShell.Streams.Error)
                        {
                            AddErrorInfo(sb, err);
                        }
                        powerShell.Streams.Error.Clear();
                    }
                    else
                    {
                        foreach (var item in results)
                        {
                            sb.Append(item);
                        }
                    }
                }
                catch (System.Exception ex)
                {
                    sb.Append(ex.Message);
                }

                powerShell.Commands.Clear();
                return sb.ToString();
            }

            static PowerShell _powerShell;

            static PowerShell powerShell
            {
                get
                {
                    if (_powerShell == null)
                    {
                        _powerShell = PowerShell.Create();
                        powerShell.Runspace = PSConfig.GetPSConfig;
                        if (!string.IsNullOrEmpty(PSConfig.Profile) &&
    File.Exists(PSConfig.Profile))
                        {
                            var script =
                              File.ReadAllText(PSConfig.Profile);
                            _powerShell.AddScript(script);
                            _powerShell.Invoke();
                            powerShell.Commands.Clear();
                        }
                    }
```

```
                return _powerShell;
            }
        }

        private static void AddErrorInfo(StringBuilder sb,
                                        ErrorRecord err)
        {
            sb.Append(err.ToString());
            sb.AppendFormat("\r\n   +{0}",
                err.InvocationInfo.PositionMessage);
            sb.AppendFormat("\r\n   + CategoryInfo          :{0}",
                err.CategoryInfo);
            sb.AppendFormat("\r\n   + FullyQualifiedErrorId :{0}",
                err.FullyQualifiedErrorId.ToString());
            sb.AppendLine();
        }
    }
}
```

PSConfig.cs

```
namespace EmbeddedPSConsole
{
    public class PSConfig
    {
        private static string _profile;
        private static Runspace _rs;

        public static Runspace GetPSConfig { get { return rs; } }

        public static string Profile
        {
            get
            {
                return _profile;
            }
            set
            {
                _profile = value;

                AddVariable("profile",
    System.IO.Path.Combine(Environment.CurrentDirectory, _profile));
                PS.ExecutePS("$a='Executes so the profile is loaded.'");
            }
        }

        private static Runspace rs
        {
            get
            {
                if (_rs == null)
                {
                    _rs = RunspaceFactory.CreateRunspace();
                    _rs.ThreadOptions =
```

```
                    PSThreadOptions.UseCurrentThread;
                _rs.Open();

                return _rs;
            }
            return _rs;
        }
    }

    public static void AddVariable(string name, object value)
    {
        rs.SessionStateProxy.SetVariable(name, value);
    }
}
}
```

Summary

So that's the walkthrough of the Beaver Music application. Surfacing the internals of your application provides numerous benefits to you, your team, and your client. And because PowerShell is based on .NET, this process is virtually seamless.

Providing a scripting language for an application is not a new idea. Perhaps you've heard of Visual Basic for Applications (*http://bit.ly/44PKAt*)? This language is built into most Microsoft applications. In Microsoft Excel, for example, you can record activities and then save the VBA scripts for later use.

Companies like Autodesk (*http://usa.autodesk.com/*), a world leader in 3D design software, also offer VBA as an embedded scripting language for their products.

In the gaming industry, Lua (*http://www.lua.org/*) is the scripting language used by World of Warcraft developer Blizzard Entertainment for interface customization (*http://www.wowwiki.com/Lua*). Blizzard has been using scripting languages to augment its offerings for decades. We should follow its lead as quickly as we can.

Why is PowerShell preferred over, say, VBA, IronPython, or IronRuby? These are excellent choices for their dynamic capabilities, but PowerShell is just as programmable, and it is tuned differently. For example:

```
Get-ChildItem |
    Sort LastWriteTime -Descending |
    Select FullName
```

Mirroring this in those other languages is a challenge. Extending it as simply as it can be done in PowerShell? Difficult at best.

PowerShell also provides common functions like sorting, filtering, grouping, formatting, outputting, and more. And, given PowerShell's growing integration with the rest of the Windows platform, as PowerShell grows, *so does your application*.

## CHAPTER 6

PowerShell and the Internet

PowerShell interacts really well with the Web—it's able to access files, XML, JSON, web services, and more directly from the Internet. PowerShell does not have cURL (*http://bit.ly/9mSnL7*) or GNU Wget (*http://bit.ly/XAhQh*) support out of the box, but because it is an amazing glue language that is deeply integrated with the .NET Framework, one area where its capabilities really shine is in connecting a set of powerful underlying components. PowerShell v3 makes this even easier using the cmdlets `Invoke-WebRequest`, `Invoke-RestMethod`, `ConvertTo-Json`, and `ConvertFrom-Json`.

It's interesting to note that, even though PowerShell was envisioned over a decade ago and v2 was delivered back in 2009, it is able to keep pace with daily development needs.

Taking advantage over the Web of something like JavaScript Object Notation (JSON; *http://bit.ly/1HwvBY*), a lightweight data-interchange format, is easy using .NET libraries designed to parse it and present it in a way that's consumable by PowerShell.

In this chapter, I'll demonstrate code that will let you pull down differently formatted information from websites. The amount of public information available is enormous. Contributed by individuals, companies, and governments, these huge datasets can give us insight into myriad subjects and can be easily accessed via PowerShell.

Net.WebClient

One cool PowerShell demo I like to give is showing how to pull down the details of a blog's RSS feed (*http://bit.ly/QWNVt*) in just three lines of code:

```
$url  = "http://feeds.feedburner.com/DevelopmentInABlink"
$feed = (New-Object Net.WebClient).DownloadString($url)
([xml]$feed).rss.channel.item | Select title, pubDate
```

This simple code gives us the following:

```
title                                            pubDate
-----                                            -------
Using PowerShell to solve Project Euler: Problem 1    Sun, 08 Jan
PowerShell and IEnumerable<T>                         Sat, 24 Dec
```

```
PowerShell, Windows Azure and Node.js              Sat, 17 Dec
How to find the second to last Friday in December - Usin... Sat, 17 Dec
PowerShell - Using the New York Times Semantic Web APIs  Sun, 04 Dec
My First PowerShell V3 ISE Add-on                  Sun, 04 Dec
Use PowerShell V3 to Find Out About Your Twitter Followers Thu, 24 Nov
```

Using the `Net.WebClient` class from the .NET Framework, the `DownloadString()` method retrieves the RSS as a string. Next, using the PowerShell XML accelerator, `[xml]`, we transform the data in the `$feed` variable into an `XmlDocument` and dot-notate over it to get to the item details. Piping this to `Select`, we pull out just the `title` and `pubDate`.

Wrapping Code in a PowerShell Function

Good PowerShell script discipline is to wrap snippets like the preceding example in functions. It helps organize your code and makes it composable.

```
function Get-WebData {

    param([string]$Url, [Switch]$Raw)

    $wc   = New-Object Net.WebClient
    $feed = $wc.DownloadString($Url)

    if($Raw) { return $feed }

    [xml]$feed
}
```

`Get-WebData` takes two parameters: the `$Url`, which is the resource on the site you're accessing, and `$Raw`. If you don't specify `$Raw`, `Get-WebData` tries to accelerate the string returned from the site as an `XmlDocument`.

```
$url = "http://feeds.feedburner.com/DevelopmentInABlink"
(Get-WebData $url).rss.channel.item |
    select title, pubDate
```

PowerShell v3 adds a number of new functions. Later in this chapter, in "Invoke-Rest-Method" on page 88, you'll see one such function that obsoletes a function like `Get-WebData` and has more capability.

Reading CSV-Formatted Data from the Web

Retrieving the contents of a file containing data in the CSV format requires the `-Raw` parameter on the `Get-WebData` function:

```
$url = "http://dougfinke.com/PowerShellForDevelopers/albums.csv"
(Get-WebData $url -Raw) | ConvertFrom-Csv
```

Here are the results:

```
Artist                                  Name
------                                  ----
Michael Jackson                         Thriller
AC/DC                                   Back in Black
Pink Floyd                              The Dark Side of the Moon
Whitney Houston / Various artists The Bodyguard
Meat Loaf                               Bat Out of Hell
Eagles                                  Their Greatest Hits
Various artists                         Dirty Dancing
Backstreet Boys                         Millennium
```

The results can then be piped to the PowerShell cmdlet `ConvertFrom-Csv`, which transforms that data into an array of PowerShell objects with properties.

Reading XML-Formatted Data from the Web

Retrieving the contents of a file containing XML is easy using the `Get-WebData` function:

```
$url = "http://dougfinke.com/PowerShellForDevelopers/albums.xml"
(Get-WebData $url).albums.album
```

Dot-notating through nodes in the results transforms that data into an array of PowerShell objects with properties.

The Structure of XML Data

Following is a snippet of the XML we read with the `Get-WebData` call in the preceding PowerShell script. The structure and the dot notation used in that script enable us to loop through all the data simply using `albums.album`.

```
<albums>
  <album>
    <artist>Michael Jackson</artist>
    <name>Thriller</name>
  </album>
  <album>
    <artist>AC/DC</artist>
    <name>Back in Black</name>
  </album>
<albums>
```

Here is the XML transformed into PowerShell objects:

```
Artist                   Name
------                   ----
Michael Jackson          Thriller
AC/DC                    Back in Black
```

US Government Data Sources

Here we're accessing the US Consumer Product Safety Commission site and pulling down product recall information stored in an XML format:

```
$url = "http://www.cpsc.gov/cpscpub/prerel/prerel.xml"
(Get-WebData $url).rss.channel.item
```

Data acquisition couldn't be easier:

```
title       : Uni-O Industries Recalls O-Grill Portable Gas Grills
description : The regulator on the grill can leak gas which can ignite
pubDate     : Tue, 03 Jan 2012 16:00:00 GMT
link        : http://www.cpsc.gov/cpscpub/prerel/prhtml12/12077.html
```

The US Government has an entire index of publicly available data (*http://bit.ly/ kR1wZ*) accessible through both web services and XML. Google around for other free public resources—if you can think of it, someone has put it on the Internet.

Invoke-RestMethod

Invoke-RestMethod is a new PowerShell v3 cmdlet. It simplifies how you can work with the Web. Invoke-RestMethod is available to you without your having to dot-source other scripts or import a module.

```
$url = "http://dougfinke.com/PowerShellForDevelopers/albums.csv"
Invoke-RestMethod $url | ConvertFrom-Csv
```

That means you can deliver a script to another user who has PowerShell v3 installed, and you're good to go. Using Get-WebData, you need to either deliver the extra script file or copy and paste that code into scripts you distribute. Plus, you then own the Get-WebData function, testing, enhancing, and upgrading.

But wait—there's more. In the next two sections, we'll take advantage of Invoke-Rest Method's –ReturnType parameter, which defaults to Detect.

Detecting XML

Invoke-RestMethod does a lot for us. Like the (New-Object Net.WebClient).Download String(), it retrieves the content file. Then it goes a step further, autodetecting that the content is XML and returning an XmlDocument. The –ReturnType takes three values: Detect, Xml, and Json.

```
$url = "http://dougfinke.com/PowerShellForDevelopers/albums.xml"
(Invoke-RestMethod $url).albums.album
```

If you know the type of data you're going after, you can short-circuit the detection process.

Detecting JSON

Let's retrieve the same album data, except now it's stored in JSON format. We use the same approach as retrieving the XML data. This time, through, `Invoke-RestMethod` detects the JSON format and automatically converts the JSON into an array of objects of type `PSCustomObject` with the properties `Artist` and `Name`.

```
$url = "http://dougfinke.com/PowerShellForDevelopers/albums.js"
Invoke-RestMethod $url
```

Following is a sample of the returned data. This output will be identical whether the XML or JSON format is returned. This means you can meld the same data across multiple websites with different formats and produce a uniform output. Pretty powerful!

```
Artist                                  Name
------                                  ----
Michael Jackson                         Thriller
AC/DC                                   Back in Black
Pink Floyd                              The Dark Side of the Moon
Whitney Houston / Various artists       The Bodyguard
Meat Loaf                               Bat Out of Hell
Eagles                                  Their Greatest Hits
Various artists                         Dirty Dancing
Backstreet Boys                         Millennium
Bee Gees / Various artists              Saturday Night Fever
Fleetwood Mac                           Rumours
Shania Twain                            Come On Over
```

We've now walked through some of the key building blocks for interacting with data on the Web. These data interchange formats are universal. Next we'll cover some more interesting applications of the same approach.

PowerShell and The *New York Times* Semantic API

With the *New York Times* Semantic API (*http://bit.ly/FIIIQ*), you get access to the long list of people, places, organizations, and other locations, entities, and descriptors that make up the controlled vocabulary used as metadata by the *New York Times*—sometimes referred to as "Times Tags" and used for Times Topics pages (*http://nyti.ms/ybl23p*).

```
Get-SemanticNYT "Obama" |
    Get-SemanticNYTArticles |
    Where links |
        Select -ExpandProperty article_list |
        Select -ExpandProperty results |
        Select date, title, url |
        Out-GridView
```

Figure 6-1. Retrieving articles from the New York Times

This script works only in PowerShell v3. We are retrieving the information in JSON format using the Semantic API and `Invoke-RestMethod`. Figure 6-1 shows the results piped to `Out-GridView`.

Reading The *New York Times*, part 1

```
function Get-SemanticNYT {

    param($query = "obama")

    $uri = "http://api.nytimes.com/svc/semantic/v2/"+
        "concept/search.json?query=$query&api-key=$apiKey"

    (Invoke-RestMethod $uri).results
}
```

Reading The *New York Times*, part 2

```
function Get-SemanticNYTArticles {

    param(
        [Parameter(ValueFromPipelineByPropertyName=$true)]
        $concept_name,
        [Parameter(ValueFromPipelineByPropertyName=$true)]
        $concept_type
    )

    Process {
      $uri = "http://api.nytimes.com/svc/semantic/v2/" +
      "concept/name/$concept_type/$concept_name.json?&" +
      "fields=all&api-key=$apiKey"
```

```
        (Invoke-RestMethod $uri).results
    }
}
```

The two PowerShell v3 functions used in these examples, `Get-SemanticNYT` and `Get-SemanticNYIArticles`, are simple wrappers used to construct *New York Times* URLs correctly. These are passed to the `Invoke-RestMethod` cmdlet, which does the heavy lifting of connecting to the site, pulling down the JSON, and transforming it to PowerShell arrays.

`Get-SemanticNYTArticles` makes use of `ValueFromPipelineByPropertyName` and the `Process` block.

`ValueFromPipelineByPropertyName` indicates that the parameter can take values from a property of the incoming pipeline object that has the same name as this parameter. This means there is a property called `concept_name` and `concept_type` emitted from the `Get-SemanticNYT` function. When we pipe `Get-SemanticNYT` to `Get-SemanticNYTArticles`, we leverage PowerShell's parameter binding mechanism. This is one of the "essence enabling" features of PowerShell. Each item from `Get-SemanticNYT` is automatically passed through the pipeline, and the properties `concept_name` and `concept_type` are bound to the same-named parameters in `Get-SemanticNYTArticles`.

The `Process` block handles iterating over the data piped, doing the move next and checking for end of stream. This frees us up to create solutions and worry less about the mechanics of passing parameters properly.

In less than three-quarters of a page of PowerShell v3 code, we're querying web-based articles from the *New York Times* via its Semantic API, handling a web REST interaction, transforming JSON to PowerShell (.NET) objects, and finally displaying the results in a WPF GUI.

These are powerful components that developers can easily add to their toolbox.

New-WebServiceProxy

The `New-WebServiceProxy` cmdlet creates a web service proxy object that lets you use and manage the web service in Windows PowerShell. Let's take a look next at how we can leverage this tool to read some ticker information about stock symbols.

Stock WebService

There are many sites available that provide stock quotes. This means we need to navigate to the desired page, type in the symbol, press Enter, and then read the information. What if I want to check several symbols? What if I check stocks every few minutes? Maybe I want to save the stock information details. Even better, say I want to do some quick calculations on the fly. We'll use a *web service* to get this done. Web services are typically *application programming interfaces* (APIs) that are accessed via *hypertext transfer protocol* (HTTP) and executed on a remote system hosting the requested services. Web services tend to fall into one of two camps: big web services and RESTful web services.

```
function Get-Quote {
    param(
        [Parameter(ValueFromPipeline=$true)]
        [string[]]$symbol,
        [Switch]$Raw
    )

    Begin {
        $url = "http://www.webservicex.net/stockquote.asmx?wsdl"
        $proxy = New-WebServiceProxy $url
    }

    Process {
        $result = $proxy.GetQuote($symbol)

        if($Raw) { return $result }

        [xml]$result
    }
}

"IBM", "AAPL", "GM", "GE", "MSFT", "GOOG" |
    Get-Quote |
    ForEach {$_.StockQuotes.Stock} |
    Format-Table
```

In this example, we easily retrieve data for several stock symbols in a single call.

The `New-WebServiceProxy`, inside the `Begin` block, executes only the first time through the function and creates a web service proxy object that lets you use and manage the web service in PowerShell.

Then, in the `Process` block, executed for each item in the pipeline, the `GetQuote()` method is called, passing in the `$symbol`. `GetQuote` returns an XML data source, so using the `[xml]` accelerator returns an `XmlDocument` for each symbol that is located.

Dig a Little Deeper

`New-WebServiceProxy` creates a web service proxy object that lets you use and manage a web service in PowerShell. It retrieves the Web Service Definition Language (WSDL), and on the fly generates and compiles an object that represents all the methods and parameters that you can access for that service.

The preceding example used the `GetQuote()` method, which takes a *symbol*—a string. For example, `IBM` returns an XML string containing lots of good information about that stock symbol.

Here is the shape of the XML returned by the GetQuote() method—a Stock node inside a StockQuotes node:

```
<StockQuotes>
    <Stock>
        <Symbol>IBM</Symbol>
        <Last>193.35</Last>
        <Date>2/7/2012</Date>
        <Time>4:01pm</Time>
        <Change>+0.53</Change>
        <Open>192.45</Open>
        <High>194.14</High>
        <Low>191.97</Low>
        <Volume>3432953</Volume>
        <MktCap>224.3B</MktCap>
        <PreviousClose>192.82</PreviousClose>
        <PercentageChange>+0.27%</PercentageChange>
        <AnnRange>151.71 - 194.90</AnnRange>
        <Earns>13.06</Earns>
        <P-E>14.76</P-E>
        <Name>International Bus</Name>
    </Stock>
</StockQuotes>
```

Then we pipe the XML to ForEach to pull out the actual data from $_.Stock Quotes.Stock:

```
Symbol      Last      Date        Time      Change    Open
------      ----      ----        ----      ------    ----
IBM         180.52    1/19/2012   4:02pm    -0.55     181.79
AAPL        427.75    1/19/2012   4:00pm    -1.36     430.03
GM          24.82     1/19/2012   4:00pm    +0.31     24.65
GF          19.15     1/19/2012   4:00pm    +0.13     19.03
MSFT        28.12     1/19/2012   4:00pm    -0.11     28.15
GOOG        639.57    1/19/2012   4:00pm    +6.66     640.97
```

Being able to get a proxy to a web service in a single line of PowerShell enables many scenarios—for example, quick integration testing. Here you could easily query stock symbols with known values and test to see if they are correct. Don't forget, once the data is pulled from the web service and in the pipeline, you can pipe it or transform it to another data format and save it to disk for later use.

Invoke-WebRequest

The Invoke-WebRequest cmdlet is another workhorse for integrating the Web into PowerShell. It lets you grab web pages and capture data about them; for example, when it's used with the AllElements property, you can search for HTML elements with a certain class name.

Again, Invoke-WebRequest is available out of the box with PowerShell v3. That means you can write scripts that mash up, scrape, and do significant text manipulation of any of your favorite websites. It makes capturing and scrubbing data a simple operation.

```
Flight Status for Delta Air Lines 269
On-time                                                    arrives in 25 minutes
Departure   JFK            8:04am   (was 8:05am)          Terminal 3
            New York       Jan 20                              Gate 3

Arrival     ATL            10:41am (was 10:45am)          Terminal N
            Atlanta        Jan 20                             Gate C51

On-time                                                  departs in 7 hours 24 minutes
Departure   TLV            12:40am                        Terminal 3
            Tel Aviv-Yafo  Jan 21                             Gate B7

Arrival     JFK            5:50am                         Terminal 4
            New York       Jan 21                             Gate B22

Updated 3 minutes ago by flightstats.com - Details
```

Figure 6-2. Results of the flight status

Next up, I present a couple of scripts using this cmdlet to query Google and Bing about the status of a flight. What is really cool is how few lines of code we need to do this. This is another good example of how PowerShell's composability can really light the way for useful, interesting applications.

One key addition to PowerShell v3 is the `workflow` keyword. Underneath, it is using Microsoft Workflow 4.0. In addition, the `ForEach` sprouts a new parameter in this context, `-Parallel`. Gluing together parallel workflow capabilities and easy web integration makes a powerful recipe for data acquisition.

PowerShell and Google

Say we want to find out the flight status for Delta Air flight 269; we surf to Google and type **flight status for dl 269** (see Figure 6-2).

```
function Get-FlightStatus {
    param($query="dl269")

    $url = "https://www.google.com/search?q=flight status for $query"
    $result = Invoke-WebRequest $url
    $result.AllElements |
        Where Class -eq "obcontainer" |
        Select -ExpandProperty innerText
}

Get-FlightStatus
```

In the preceding code, we type **Get-FlightStatus** at a command line and scrape the Google page using `Invoke-WebRequest`. These results have been truncated for readability:

```
Flight Status for Delta Air Lines 269
```

```
On-timearrives in 25 minutes
DepartureJFK8:04am(was 8:05am)Terminal 3
New YorkJan 20Gate 3

Updated 3 minutes ago by flightstats.com - Details
```

The key to scraping pages this way is to find an element that can be as close to uniquely identified as possible. By navigating to the page you want to scrape and clicking "View Source," you can look at the resulting HTML and figure out if that is possible. Looking at the results from Google, I saw that the flight results were in a div with a class name obcontainer. That translates to Where Class -eq "obcontainer".

The target HTML

Using Invoke-WebRequest with the where cmdlet makes quick work of scraping websites. Here is the HTML I searched to find a class name equal to obcontainer:

```html
<div class="obcontainer" style="padding-bottom:5px;">
  <div>
    <div>
      <table style="width:34.24em;border-top:0">
        <tr>
          <td >Flight Status for <b>Delta Air Lines 269</b></td>
        </tr>
      </table>
    </div>
    <div>
      <table >
        <tr>
          <td>Updated 3 minutes ago by flightstats.com - <a href=
          class=" fl">Details</a></td>
        </tr>
      </table>
    </div>
  </div>
</div>
```

So, you retrieve the web page with Invoke-WebRequest, filter AllElements by the "key" you are looking for, and select the inner text, and you're done.

Not all web pages will be this simple, but it is worth investing a few minutes to potentially unlock a data mining opportunity.

PowerShell and Bing

Here is the same query from the preceding Google example, now in Bing:

```
function Get-FlightStatus {
    param($query="dl269")

    $url = "http://bing.com?q=flight status for $query"

    $result = Invoke-WebRequest $url
```

```
    $result.AllElements |
        Where Class -eq "ans" |
        Select -First 1 -ExpandProperty innerText
}
```

The two differences are the "key" to filter on in the `Where` cmdlet, and the `-First 1` parameter found on the `Select` cmdlet, which we need to use because Bing returns several answers and we want the first one.

```
Flight status for Delta 269
Landed early · Jan 20, 2012
From: New York (JFK) 08:04 AM (was 08:05 AM) · gate 3, terminal 3 · map
To: Atlanta (ATL) 10:33 AM (was 10:45 AM) · gate C51, terminal N · map
Other flight segments · TLV-JFK

Data provided by Bing Travel · Source: www.flightstats.com, 2 minutes ago
```

Overall, this is a very clean and simple approach for querying search engines and pulling out just the details you need. Even better, it is not limited to just query engines—you can use it for any public data on the Web.

PowerShell and the Twitter API

As you probably already know, Twitter is an information network and communication mechanism that produces more than 200 million "tweets" (status updates) a day. The Twitter platform offers access to that data through its APIs. Each API represents a facet of Twitter, and allows developers to build upon and extend their applications in new and creative ways.

By tapping into the Twitter search API to search for one of my favorite topics—PowerShell—and then leveraging the `Get-WebData` function presented earlier, we can easily extract the title and author of tweets containing the word "PowerShell."

```
. .\Get-WebData.ps1
$result = Get-WebData "http://search.twitter.com/search.rss?q=PowerShell"
$result.rss.channel.item |
    Select title, author
```

The resulting XML returned by the Twitter search API is far richer than just the `title` and `author` fields, however. It contains a link to the image the author uses, the date of the tweet, a link to the original tweet, and more. Plus, this is only the search API. Twitter supports many more APIs; for an example, check out my blog post "Use PowerShell V3 to Find Out About Your Twitter Followers" (*http://bit.ly/tJPhoO*).

```
title                          author
-----                          ------
I heart #Powershell. What else ... awanderingmind@twitter.com (Jo...
I hate you people. No, not you.... billinkc@twitter.com (Bill Fel...
#PowerShell Mailbox name not al... ihunger@twitter.com (Jim Hofer)
nothing like writing #PowerShel... Josh_Atwell@twitter.com (Josh ...
#PowerShell Granting permission... ihunger@twitter.com (Jim Hofer)
```

```
NewPost:: PowerShell, Active Se...    jbmurphy@twitter.com (Jeffrey ...
Configure Git in PowerShell So ...    JohnBubriski@twitter.com (John...
Article #5 of 7 for Hey Scripti...    proxb@twitter.com (Boe Prox)
Get Powershell to wait for an S...    stackfeed@twitter.com (StackOv...
RT @PowerShellGroup: UK PowerSh...    OliverZofic@twitter.com (Olive...
GPP Registry Item Level Targeti...    AGoodies@twitter.com (A Goodies)
wadehel is windows powershell m...    pimapimapima@twitter.com (Adri...
RT @PowerShellGroup: UK PowerSh...    ScriptingGuys@twitter.com (MSF...
RT @toenuff: Revert the  #power...    ScriptingGuys@twitter.com (MSF...
The future of Exchange administ...    alexandair@twitter.com (Aleksa...
```

Many websites support similar APIs, and I strongly encourage you to investigate PowerShell as a way to rapidly tap into them, which will open up opportunities to quickly mine data from a single source or across many.

PowerShell v3 ups the game further by natively supporting cmdlets like `Invoke-WebRequest` and `Invoke-RestMethod`, which let me concentrate on the essence of data interaction across heterogeneous data stores on the Web.

Unlike ceremonial versions of web interaction—where I need to handle requests, responses, data conversions, and more—with `Invoke-RestMethod`, I pass a URL, and if it is XML or JSON on the other end, I don't even know it. I'm simply working with an array of objects with properties; piping them to other PowerShell cmdlets for sorting, grouping, slicing, and dicing; or using the intermediate results to do lookups through other APIs or on completely different sites.

Summary

We've covered a lot in this chapter. You saw how easy it is to integrate PowerShell with the Web to pull down the contents of files in three different formats: CSV, XML, and JSON. Then, you learned how to convert them on the fly to .NET (PowerShell) objects and did some analysis on the files. Finally, we pulled down entire web pages and filtered out key details based on HTML tag names.

Now you have to check out the next chapter, where I'll expand on the Twitter code and introduce you to WPF programming using only PowerShell. That's right—no XAML[1], C#.

---

1. XAML, or the Extensible Application Markup Language, is a declarative XML-based language created by Microsoft and is used for building WPF applications.

Building GUI Applications in PowerShell

When Jeffrey Snover was showing PowerShell (then Monad) around Microsoft, one of the responses he received was, "A new command line? Snover, what about Windows don't you get?" In fact, Windows Server 8 is all about not running graphical user interfaces (GUIs). It can be run as a headless server.

 Want to follow along with the examples in this chapter? Download ShowUI and you can try out the examples as you go: *http://showui.co deplex.com/*.

ShowUI is a PowerShell module to help build WPF user interfaces in script. It makes the complicated world of WPF easy to use in PowerShell. You can use ShowUI to write simple WPF gadgets, quick frontends for your scripts, components, and full applications.

Why a Chapter About GUIs?

So why a whole chapter devoted to GUIs, you ask? Great question! First off, GUIs are optimal in many scenarios. For example, sometimes users want to see a list of information that has several attributes. They don't want to see those details whizzing by on the console; they want to capture it in a screen to be able to vertically and horizontally scroll through it.

The challenge with GUIs comes when users need to do a task over and over, clicking through a number of screens, entering info, clicking some more, type, click, type, clickety, click, click. They're out!

Ultimately, as developers we need to deliver what the user wants, and that deliverable is sometimes a GUI. Being the lazy coder, I like to get my job done in the fewest lines of code possible. It's quicker, easier, less error prone, simpler to maintain, and agile.

Figure 7-1. ShowUI Hello World

Figure 7-2. PowerShell WinForms

Answer: Two Lines of Code

How many lines of PowerShell are needed to create a complete working WPF application? Two! Here's the code that yields the result shown in Figure 7-1.

```
Import-Module ShowUI
Label "Hello World" -FontSize 42 -Show
```

It'll take you more using statements, an IDE, and a compilation step to get the equivalent in C#. Here, you press Enter at the end of the second line of PowerShell code and, boom, you're done—a running WPF app.

I'll be going deeper into building PowerShell WPF applications in this chapter, but if you want another angle on using PowerShell to develop WPF applications, check out my MSDN article, "Secrets to Building a WPF Application in Windows PowerShell," at *http://msdn.microsoft.com/en-us/magazine/hh288074.aspx*.

In this chapter, you'll see a couple of full WPF applications leveraging ShowUI (which, as noted earlier, is a PowerShell module to help build WPF user interfaces in script): a Twitter search GUI and a video player. First, let's code up a GUI using WinForms.

PowerShell and WinForms

PowerShell works with WinForms out of the box. Figure 7-2 shows a simple WinForms GUI with a button; click the button, and the date will print in the console.

This PowerShell script has some lines of code worth noting. First up, a PowerShell session does not automatically load the System.Windows.Forms DLL, so we use the Add-Type -AssemblyName System.Windows.Forms method to do so.

If you use PowerShell and WinForms this way, there is no built-in editor to lay out your forms, so you need to manually handle position, sizing, and event hookup.

SAPIEN Technologies has a tool called PrimalForms (*http://www.sapien*
.com/software/primalforms) that works like the Visual Basic Forms
Editor. It lets you drag and drop controls on a designer, hook up events
by double-clicking the controls, and so on. The final result is all PowerShell.

After creating the form, we set its size and start position. Then we create a Windows
button, wire up the click event by calling the add_click() method, and pass it a PowerShell script block. We let the button's size take the default and then we add the button
to the form's Controls collection. Finally, we call the ShowDialog() method on the form,
and it displays on the screen.

```
Add-Type -AssemblyName System.Windows.Forms

$form = New-Object Windows.Forms.Form
$form.Size = New-Object Drawing.Size @(200,100)

$form.StartPosition = "CenterScreen"

$btn = New-Object System.Windows.Forms.Button
$btn.add_click({Get-Date|Out-Host})
$btn.Text = "Click here"

$form.Controls.Add($btn)
$drc = $form.ShowDialog()
```

Using WinForms to build GUIs has its advantages. It's available on any Windows OS,
so you could email a script to someone, and that person could run it and have a GUI
ready to go.

Next up, I'll use the ShowUI module, which provides abstractions you cannot achieve
through pure markup.

PowerShell, ShowUI, and the Twitter API

Being able to search social media sites quickly provides a multitude of benefits. In fact,
there are companies that do this all day long, capturing details from Twitter, Facebook,
LinkedIn, and more. After collecting all of this data, they run analytics to determine
sentiment toward a product or service (*sentiment analysis*). While we won't get into
specific analysis here, I'll show you how to query Twitter using its search API, process
the XML results so we can easily work with the data in PowerShell, and then display it
in a GUI. In less than a page of PowerShell script, we can glue together WPF and the
results of a Twitter search!

When reading over this approach, keep in mind that this is not just for Twitter or social media sites with XML feeds. For example, you could use PowerShell v3 and change the *search.rss* to *search.json*. This returns a JSON string, and in PowerShell v3, you could pipe it to `ConvertFrom-Json`. This would transform the data into PowerShell objects with properties that you could wire up into the ShowUI WPF application. Most sites on the Web today return either XML or JSON. They're just low-hanging fruit, waiting for a custom interface or a mashup.

Now take a look at the `Search-Twitter` function using the search API. It accelerates the XML into an `XmlDocument` using `[xml]` and then dot-notates down to the item in the XML feed.

```
function Search-Twitter ($q = "PowerShell") {
    $wc = New-Object Net.Webclient
    $url = "http://search.twitter.com/search.rss?q=$q"
    ([xml]$wc.downloadstring($url)).rss.channel.item
}
```

Invoking the function `Search-Twitter` returns an array of objects, each with 32 properties on it. We select just two for now and look at the results.

```
Search-Twitter | select pubDate, title
```

The following is what we get back from the search for the two fields we selected. This is useful if we wanted to save this and then query it later, but there are far more interesting fields in that data—the Twitter user's image, for example—so next let's make a little Twitter GUI app instead of just looking at the raw data in this format.

```
pubDate                        title
-------                        -----
Fri, 10 Feb 2012 00:43:33 +0000 Windows PowerShell(TM) Scripting Guide
Fri, 10 Feb 2012 00:42:17 +0000 #PowerShell Use Tab Expansion in the Po
Fri, 10 Feb 2012 00:40:56 +0000 @energizedtech Captain! She canny take
Fri, 10 Feb 2012 00:37:56 +0000 Shout out to @ToddKlindt "the PowerShel
Fri, 10 Feb 2012 00:31:38 +0000 #PowerShell February PowerShell group m
Fri, 10 Feb 2012 00:29:57 +0000 RT @mattn_jp: powershell???????????????
Fri, 10 Feb 2012 00:22:32 +0000 @robinmalik: "Very excited to play arou
Fri, 10 Feb 2012 00:22:24 +0000 It seems like it is certainly going to
Fri, 10 Feb 2012 00:21:00 +0000 #PowerShell Using PowerShell v3 to cons
Fri, 10 Feb 2012 00:16:23 +0000 ????????···?????···PowerShell?????···??
Fri, 10 Feb 2012 00:16:16 +0000 Windows PowerShell v1.0: TFM, 2nd Editi
Fri, 10 Feb 2012 00:10:23 +0000 #PowerShell Windows PowerShell for Shar
Fri, 10 Feb 2012 00:08:55 +0000 Any #Powershell gurus out there that ca
Fri, 10 Feb 2012 00:08:51 +0000 ???: powershell?get-help???firefox?????
Fri, 10 Feb 2012 00:00:38 +0000 RT @ScriptingWife: R U ready for some #
```

A Twitter GUI Application

This is a simple but full-blown WPF application interacting with the Twitter search API.

As I've mentioned before, ShowUI (*http://showui.codeplex.com/*) is a PowerShell module for building WPF user interfaces in script. You can use it to write simple WPF gadgets, quick frontends for your scripts, components, and full applications.

 ShowUI is a combined effort of James Brundage, former member of the PowerShell team and founder of Start-Automating (*http://start-automating.com/*), and Joel Bennett (*http://huddledmasses.org/*) fellow PowerShell MVP. (I'm a developer on that open source project, too.) Back in late 2008, I blogged about Ruby Shoes and the start of a PowerShell version for it (*http://bit.ly/KhZR3L*). Ruby Shoes (*http://shoesrb.com/*) is a cross-platform toolkit for writing graphical apps. I liked its domain-specific language (DSL) approach and began to put together a version for WinForms. Joel commented on that post, saying he was doing the same for WPF, which became PowerBoots (*http://bit.ly/DZiK3*). On or about that time, James was surfacing his work on his WPF approach, Windows Presentation Foundation PowerShell ToolKit (WPK). WPK is a hat tip to Tcl/Tk, a popular UNIX scripting tool, and was released as part of PowerShellPack (*http://bit.ly/dFVpfL*). Check it out—it has other great resources. ShowUI is the evolution of the two PowerShell modules PowerBoots and WPK.

Compared to C# and XAML, there is much less to learn in order to use PowerShell and ShowUI. Plus, within just a few hours of learning ShowUI, you can create interesting and useful user interfaces.

PowerShell allows a higher-level abstraction than system languages, enabling more rapid application development. ShowUI enables the same level of abstractions for creating WPF user interfaces.

The Code

These 29 lines of PowerShell (less than a page of code) produce Figure 7-3. The Search-Twitter function returns an array of PowerShell objects with properties from the Twitter query. From that data, we extract the text of the tweet and the URL pointing to the Twitter user's profile image.

If you look closely at the PowerShell code here, you'll see no loops at all. ShowUI supports WPF's data binding capabilities as well as its templating features.

```
Import-Module .\ShowUI

function Search-Twitter ($q) {
    $wc = New-Object Net.Webclient
    $url = "http://search.twitter.com/search.rss?q=$q"
```

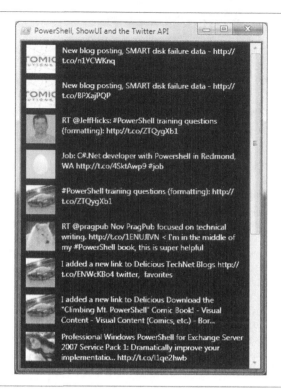

Figure 7-3. PowerShell, ShowUI, and the Twitter API

```
        ([xml]$wc.downloadstring($url)).rss.channel.item | select *
}

$ws = @{
    WindowStartupLocation = "CenterScreen"
    Width  = 500
    Height = 500
}

New-Window @ws -Show {
    ListBox -Background Black -ItemTemplate {
        Grid -Columns 55, 300 {
            Image -Column 0 -Name Image -Margin 5
            TextBlock -Column 1 -Name Title `
                -Margin 5 `
                -Foreground White `
                -TextWrapping Wrap
        } | ConvertTo-DataTemplate -Binding @{
            "Image.Source" = "image_link"
            "Title.Text" = "title"
        }
    } -ItemsSource (Search-Twitter PowerShell)
}
```

ShowUI uses a code generation technique that wraps all the WPF presentation components and their parameters so they fit seamlessly into the PowerShell ecosystem. In this code, we're accessing five WPF controls: Window, ListBox, Grid, Image, and Text Block.

We set the results of the Twitter search to the ItemsSource property of the ListBox and then let data binding take care of the rest. The ConvertTo-DataTemplate "reaches" into the data context of the control in order to find the image_link and title properties.

To do the styling, we use the -ItemTemplate parameter and ConvertTo-DataTemplate function. -ItemTemplate takes a PowerShell script block, in which we define a WPF Grid with two columns. The first column will hold an Image control, which shows the Twitter user's picture. If you set the source of the Image control to a URL, the picture is automatically fetched and displayed. The second column holds the TextBlock where the actual tweet message is displayed.

The WPF data templating model provides you with great flexibility to define the presentation of your data. WPF controls have built-in functionality to support the customization of data presentation. They give you a very flexible and powerful solution to replace the visual appearance of a data item in a control like ListBox.

ShowUI integrates with this styling functionality via the -ItemTemplate parameter and ConvertTo-DataTemplate function.

We pipe the Grid "construction" to the ConvertTo-DataTemplate function that ships with ShowUI. This is where the controls are data bound to the Twitter results created in the DataContext parameter via the -binding parameter.

If you inspect the raw data returned from Search-Twitter, you'll see that there are in fact two properties on every object, one named image_link and the other text.

Running the script bubbles up all the data into the ListBox, which is hosted by the New-Window, and we get the neat Twitter application in Figure 7-3.

ShowUI Video Player

ShowUI ships with a number of great examples, and both James Brundage and Joel Bennett have blogged and recorded videos demoing ShowUI in action. Definitely check out these links to the videos:

- My ShowUI videos (*http://vimeo.com/user7416310/videos*)
- Show CodePlex page for videos (*http://showui.codeplex.com/documentation*)
- YouTube (*http://bit.ly/MhcZbG*)

One more simple and powerful app that you can code is a GUI video player that supports drag and drop and runs as a standalone application with only a handful of script.

```
Import-Module ShowUI

New-Window -AllowDrop -On_Drop {

    $VideoPlayer.Source = @($_.Data.GetFileDropList())[0]
    $VideoPlayer.Play()
} -On_Loaded {

    $VideoPlayer.Source = Get-ChildItem -Path `
      "$env:Public\Videos\Sample Videos" -Filter *.wmv |
      Get-Random | Select-Object -ExpandProperty Fullname
    $VideoPlayer.Play()
} -On_Closing {

    $VideoPlayer.Stop()
} -Content {

    New-MediaElement -Name VideoPlayer -LoadedBehavior Manual
} -AsJob
```

New-Window creates a WPF window, and then -AsJob runs the window as a background job. Launching this window from the PowerShell console runs this application without blocking the command line from doing more work.

The window gets the video player embedded in the -Content parameter, and it is named VideoPlayer. ShowUI makes that name accessible as $VideoPlayer. You can see this name being used in the rest of the script for properties being set, Source, and methods being called, Play() and Stop().

The -AllowDrop parameter enables the window as a drop target. You can drag other videos to the surface and drop them, and they will play. The -On_Drop parameter wires up the drop event, reads and sets the file dropped to the video player, and plays it.

The -On_Loaded event is called when the window initially loads and a random *.wmv* file is selected to be played. Finally, when the window is closed, the –On_Closing event is called, and Stop() terminates the playing video.

Notice how it takes more space to explain a ShowUI application than it does to write it!

Summary

GUIs are fundamentally gluing applications; they don't really create new functionality, but rather they make connections between controls and the internal functions of an application.

Scripting languages excel at gluing. ShowUI connects the underlying components of WPF and PowerShell to create an environment of exceptional power. Using PowerShell this way is not limited to wrapping WPF and GUI components, however; with this approach, you can develop applications five to ten times faster.

PowerShell is not a replacement for a system programming language or vice versa. Each is suited to solve different problems. Finding that division of labor and combining their strengths leads to more rapid development and more flexible approaches.

CHAPTER 8

DLLs, Types, Properties, Methods, and Microsoft Roslyn

How do you learn to work with PowerShell, the .NET Framework, your .NET DLLs, third-party .NET DLLs, and other Microsoft and non-Microsoft libraries? In this chapter, I'll step you through how to load DLLs and discover the types, properties, and methods that you can call during a live interactive session.

When you're working with the .NET Framework, your best friend is the MSDN Library (*http://msdn.microsoft.com/en-us/library/*). It's an essential source of information for developers using Microsoft tools, products, technologies, and services.

For example, if I search for "programmatically put data on the clipboard MSDN," I find the page "Clipboard Class (System.Windows)" (*http://bit.ly/GJuNcS*). This page details all the information I need—specifically the assembly needed to load (`PresentationCore`), the fully qualified type name (namespace and class) needed to call `System.Windows.Clipboard`, and a list of the methods that are available to use.

Sending Text to the Clipboard

To kick this section off, we'll create a PowerShell function to put the text "Hello World" on the clipboard. I'll show you how to use `Get-Member` to list out method names at the command line so you can discover them in your current session. This is a convenient technique that can speed development when you need to find out what methods exist on an object you are using.

For this example, if you are using PowerShell v2 you'll need to start with the command-line switch -STA; this starts the shell using a *single-threaded apartment*. While the PowerShell v3 apartment state defaults to STA, the PowerShell v2 apartment state defaults instead to MTA (*multi-threaded apartment*).

We need this switch because we'll be using the clipboard from WPF, and it requires an STA thread.

For more background, check out "Why does WPF require a STAThread attribute to be applied to the Main method?" at *http://bit.ly/GCBfCQ*.

Now, let's get started. First, we'll load up the WPF PresentationCore DLL into our current PowerShell session.

```
Add-Type -AssemblyName PresentationCore
```

Once this is done, we'll use Get-Member to find all the static methods on the clipboard. We can do this with any .NET assembly that is loaded into the PowerShell session.

```
[System.Windows.Clipboard] | Get-Member -Static
```

You need to wrap the type System.Windows.Clipboard in brackets ([]), as it denotes a type. That line of code produces this data:

```
   TypeName: System.Windows.Clipboard

Name                  MemberType  Definition
----                  ----------  ----------
Clear                 Method      static System.Void Clear()
ContainsAudio         Method      static bool ContainsAudio()
ContainsData          Method      static bool ContainsData(string format)
ContainsFileDropList  Method      static bool ContainsFileDropList()
ContainsImage         Method      static bool ContainsImage()
ContainsText          Method      static bool ContainsText(), static bool
GetAudioStream        Method      static System.IO.Stream GetAudioStream(
GetData               Method      static System.Object GetData(string for
GetDataObject         Method      static System.Windows.IDataObject GetDa
GetFileDropList       Method      static System.Collections.Specialized.S
GetImage              Method      static System.Windows.Media.Imaging.Bit
GetText               Method      static string GetText(), static string
IsCurrent             Method      static bool IsCurrent(System.Windows.ID
SetAudio              Method      static System.Void SetAudio(byte[] audi
SetData               Method      static System.Void SetData(string forma
SetDataObject         Method      static System.Void SetDataObject(System
SetFileDropList       Method      static System.Void SetFileDropList(Syst
SetImage              Method      static System.Void SetImage(System.Wind
SetText               Method      static System.Void SetText(string text)
```

The last method in the list, SetText(), is what we're after. We combine this all together, and we can put text on the clipboard.

```
[System.Windows.Clipboard]::SetText("Hello World")
```

Now we can launch Notepad and press Ctrl-V to paste the text. Better yet, we can wrap it in a function that can accept the parameter either from the pipeline or normally.

```
function Out-Clipboard {
    param(
        [Parameter(ValueFromPipeline=$true)]
        [string]$text
    )

    Process {
        [System.Windows.Clipboard]::SetText($text)
    }
}
```

Now, we can set text to the clipboard with either of these approaches:

```
Out-Clipboard (Get-Date)
# Or
Get-Date | Out-Clipboard
```

 As I was writing this chapter, a good friend and fellow PowerShell expert, Trevor Sullivan, posted "Copy Filenames to Clipboard with PowerShell" to his blog (*http://bit.ly/xncc7c*). Check out his implementation. You can specify a path, and the script iterates over files, selects each full name, collects them as a string array, and then copies them to the clipboard. Creative idea! Plus, PowerShell makes it easy to create solutions like this:

```
Copy-FileNamesToClipboard -Path c:\temp\docs
```

Transcoding C# to PowerShell

Here we're going to use Jonathan Creamer's C# approach (*http://bit.ly/zsAjpL*) to consuming StackOverflow's JSON API but do it in PowerShell. I find this useful because I can spot snippets of C# and transform them to PowerShell quickly, and then I have the full breadth and reach of PowerShell to make this stuff sing.

 I did a PowerShell video back in 2008 showing how to count the number of characters in an array of strings, first in C# and then whittling the code down to a single line of PowerShell. It's seven minutes worth watching and communicates the *ceremony versus essence* principle very nicely. Check it out here: *http://bit.ly/GEejQW*.

First, the C#

Jonathan wanted to get information about a StackOverflow user, badge, answer, and view counts for starters. If you check out his post, he shows the resulting JSON from the query plus the C# code that requests the data from the URL, unzips it with GZip, and then uses JSON.NET to deserialize the result into a C# object so it can be easily processed.

I want to focus on the retrieval of Jonathan's solution. The following C# snippet returns the JSON for the user 110865 (that's me). But first, here is an abbreviated view of the returned JSON:

```
{
  "user_id": 110865,
  "display_name": "Doug Finke",
  "reputation": 1696,
  "website_url": "http://dougfinke.com/blog/",
  "location": "New York, NY",
  "about_me": "Software Developer and Microsoft PowerShell MVP",
  "question_count": 7,
  "answer_count": 72,
  "view_count": 70,
  "up_vote_count": 72,
  "badge_counts": {
    "gold": 0,
    "silver": 3,
    "bronze": 9
  }
}
```

Now, let's take a look at the C# that makes this happen. By changing this to PowerShell, we can immediately reduce the ceremony by stripping out using, namespace, class, and Main.

```
using System;

namespace ConsoleApplication1
{
    class Program
    {
        static void Main(string[] args)
        {
            var url = @"http://api.stackoverflow.com/1.1/users/110865";

            var client = new System.Net.WebClient();

            var response = client.DownloadData(url);

            var decompress = new System.IO.Compression.GZipStream(
                new System.IO.MemoryStream(response),
                System.IO.Compression.CompressionMode.Decompress);

            var reader = new System.IO.StreamReader(decompress);

            Console.WriteLine(reader.ReadToEnd());
        }
    }
}
```

Intermediate PowerShell

Another step is to change the var designation to a $, and I'll also remove the @ and; (too much typing for my taste). So, a line in C# will go from this:

```
var url = @"http://api.stackoverflow.com/1.1/users/110865";
```

To this in PowerShell:

```
$url = "http://api.stackoverflow.com/1.1/users/110865"
```

Next, we'll change the C# new keyword to the PowerShell New-Object syntax. It's more straightforward. This C# code:

```
var client = new System.Net.WebClient();
```

becomes this in PowerShell:

```
$client = New-Object Net.WebClient
```

To summarize, we added a $ to client and changed new to New-Object. We no longer need the System designation, so we dropped the parentheses and semicolon. That's how you create an object in PowerShell.

I want to draw your attention to few things in the following script. The $data variable contains a byte array. The Net.WebClient is created using New-Object; it's wrapped in parentheses and can be immediately used as an object so the DownloadData() method can be invoked.

```
function Get-StackOverflowUser ($id) {

    $url = "http://api.stackoverflow.com/1.1/users/$id"
    $data = (New-Object Net.WebClient).DownloadData($url)
    $memoryStream = New-Object System.IO.MemoryStream(,$data)
    $decompress = New-Object `
        System.IO.Compression.GZipStream($memoryStream,"Decompress")
    $reader = New-Object System.IO.StreamReader($decompress)
    $ret = $reader.ReadToEnd()

    ($ret | ConvertFrom-Json).Users
}

Get-StackOverflowUser -id 110865
```

A final observation: when the GZipStream object is created, the second parameter in the constructor takes a CompressionMode enum. PowerShell lets you pass in a string and converts it to the enum for you. Ah—less ceremony, more essence.

Results

So now we have a workable PowerShell function where we can pass in a StackOver flow user ID, get the data, unzip it, get the JSON, and produce this PowerShell object with properties.

Ninety percent of this example works in PowerShell v2. We can easily transform the JSON string to a PowerShell object in PowerShell v3 using the `ConvertFrom-Json` cmdlet, as you can see in the following line:

```
($ret | ConvertFrom-Json).Users
```

Converting JSON to PowerShell

If we wanted to convert the JSON using PowerShell, we could use the same libraries Jonathan used in his C# solution. We could load up the JSON.NET DLL and call the same methods. PowerShell v3 adds several cmdlets that make working with the Web and its data a snap.

```
user_id             : 110865
display_name        : Doug Finke
reputation          : 1696
website_url         : http://dougfinke.com/blog/
location            : New York, NY
about_me            : Software Developer and Microsoft PowerShell MVP
question_count      : 7
answer_count        : 72
view_count          : 70
up_vote_count       : 72
badge_counts        : @{gold=0; silver=3; bronze=9}
```

In closing, I'd like to point out the reach of PowerShell. Using this new function, `Get-StackOverflowUser`, we can easily get user information from this website and into Microsoft Excel for analysis. Here, we retrieve the information about a `StackOverflow` user and export it to a CSV file. Using PowerShell's `Invoke-Item`, our script reads the file extension and launches Microsoft Excel.

```
Get-StackOverflowUser | Export-Csv -NoTypeInformation .\users.csv
Invoke-Item .\users.csv
```

I can't stress this point enough. Once information is in PowerShell as an object, you can do amazing things with it. Here I showed how simple it is to get it up working with Excel. Exporting the information to another REST endpoint, a web service, or SQL Server is just as easy.

Microsoft's Roslyn

In the past, compilers have acted as black boxes—meaning you put source text in, and an assembly comes out. All of the rich information that the compiler produces is thrown away and unavailable for anyone to use.

Microsoft's Roslyn project changes that traditional model by opening up the Visual Basic and C# compilers as APIs. These APIs allow tools and end users to share in the compilers' wealth of information and code analysis. The Roslyn community technology preview (CTP) gives us a taste of the next generation of language object models for code generation, analysis, and refactoring, and the upcoming support for scripting and interactive use of VB and C#.

Roslyn opens up new opportunities for developers to write powerful refactorings and language analysis tools, as well as to allow anyone to incorporate parsers, semantic engines, code generators, and scripting in their applications.

If you want to play along in this section, you need to download the Roslyn CTP (*http://www.microsoft.com/download/en/details.aspx?id=27746*) from *http://www.microsoft.com/en-us/download/details.aspx?id=27746*.

 While the amazing opportunities that Roslyn presents are too much to cover in detail here, I encourage you to check out my blog post, "Analyze C# Source files using PowerShell and the Get-RoslynInfo Cmdlet," at *http://bit.ly/v9QlAW*.

Microsoft Roslyn and PowerShell

The Roslyn libraries contain gems ready for discovery. To investigate them, we're going to use Add-Type again, but this time with two parameters: the -Path parameter, which lets us point directly to a DLL, and the -PassThru parameter, which returns a System.Runtime object that represents the types that were added.

```
$dll = "C:\Program Files\Reference Assemblies\Microsoft\Roslyn
\v1.0\Roslyn.Services.dll"

Add-Type -Path $dll -PassThru |
    Where {$_.IsPublic -And $_.BaseType} | Sort Name
```

We'll pipe this to the Where cmdlet so we can filter only the Public libraries that have a BaseType. Finally, we'll sort the results. I usually squirrel away snippets like this and wrap them in a function for easy use later. This one can be used over and over and parameterized with a Filename so we can inspect any .NET DLL.

```
IsPublic IsSerial Name                                    BaseType
-------- -------- ----                                    --------
True     False    CostBasedRetainerFactory`1              System.Object
True     False    DefaultWorkspaceListener                System.Object
True     False    DocumentId                              System.Object
True     False    DocumentInfo                            System.Object
True     False    ExportLanguageServiceAttribute          System.Compon
True     False    ExportLanguageServiceProviderAttribute  System.Compon
True     False    ExportMSBuildLanguageServiceAttribute   Roslyn.Servic
True     False    ExportWorkspaceServiceFactoryAttribute  System.Compon
True     False    Extensions                              System.Object
True     False    HostWorkspace                           Roslyn.Servic
True     False    PersistenceService                      System.Object
True     False    ProjectId                               System.Object
True     False    ProjectionWorkspace                     Roslyn.Servic
True     False    Solution                                System.Object
True     False    SolutionEdit                            System.Object
```

```
True     False    SolutionExtensions              System.Object
True     False    SolutionId                      System.Object
True     True     SymbolDescriptionGroups         System.Enum
True     True     SymbolDescriptionOptions        System.Enum
True     False    TrackingWorkspace               Roslyn.Servic
True     False    Workspace                       System.Object
True     False    WorkspaceExtensions             System.Object
True     False    WorkspaceKind                   System.Object
True     False    WorkspaceTaskSchedulerFactory   System.Object
```

The name that grabbed my attention was Solution. Let's see if it has any interesting static members we can work with.

```
[Roslyn.Services.Solution] | Get-Member -Static
```

Here is the list of static methods and properties, and a peek at their signatures:

```
   TypeName: Roslyn.Services.Solution

Name                    MemberType Definition
----                    ---------- ----------
Create                  Method     static Roslyn.Services.ISolution
Equals                  Method     static bool Equals(System.Object
HasProjects             Property   bool HasProjects {get;}
Id                      Property   Roslyn.Services.SolutionId Id {ge
Load                    Method     static Roslyn.Services.ISolution
LoadStandAloneProject   Method     static Roslyn.Services.IProject L
MetadataFileProvider    Property   Roslyn.Compilers.IMetadataFilePro
ProjectIds              Property   System.Collections.Generic.IEnume
Projects                Property   System.Collections.Generic.IEnume
ReferenceEquals         Method     static bool ReferenceEquals(Syste
```

The Load() method caught my eye here. The listing cut off the full signature; here it is in full:

```
Load(string solutionFileName, string configuration, string platform)
```

This is interesting because it looks like it'll read and parse a Visual Studio solution file. Historically, this was annoying to do on your own. Now Microsoft is making it available and will support it going forward.

Using PowerShell to Display Visual Studio Detail

Let's put the Load() method to use by pointing it to a Visual Studio solution:

```
$slnFileName = Resolve-Path "..\..\C#\BeaverMusic\BeaverMusic.sln"

[Roslyn.Services.Solution]::Load($slnFileName)
```

And we get some good details from this; let's see what's in Projects:

```
Id                   : Roslyn.Services.SolutionId
MetadataFileProvider :
HasProjects          : True
ProjectIds           : {(ProjectId, C:\O'Reilly\examples\C#\Beaver
                       (ProjectId, C:\O'Reilly\examples\C#\BeaverM
```

```
                               C:\O'Reilly\examples\C#\BeaverMusic\BeaverM
                               C:\O'Reilly\examples\C#\BeaverMusic\Embedde
          Projects          : {(ProjectId, C:\O'Reilly\examples\C#\Beaver
                               (ProjectId, C:\O'Reilly\examples\C#\BeaverM
                               C:\O'Reilly\examples\C#\BeaverMusic\BeaverM
                               C:\O'Reilly\examples\C#\BeaverMusic\Embedde
```

Here we'll pick off just the first project:

```
[Roslyn.Services.Solution]::Load($slnFileName).Projects |
    Select -First 1
```

The Roslyn API lets us get rich information on the projects and files inside a Visual Studio solution. Looking at the output of the previous command, we'll use the Documents property and pull together one more script that extracts the project name and all of the files in that project.

```
Solution                  : Roslyn.Services.Solution
Id                        : (ProjectId, C:\O'Reilly\examples\C#\
LanguageServices          : Roslyn.Services.CSharp.CSharpLanguag
AssemblyName              : BeaverMusic
DisplayName               : BeaverMusic.UI.Shell
MetadataReferences        : {Roslyn.Compilers.AssemblyFileRefere
ProjectReferences         : {(ProjectId, C:\O'Reilly\examples\C#
                             (ProjectId, C:\O'Reilly\examples\C#\
                             C:\O'Reilly\examples\C#\BeaverMusic\
CompilationOptions        : Roslyn.Compilers.CSharp.CompilationO
ParseOptions              : Roslyn.Compilers.CSharp.ParseOptions
AssemblyResolver          : Roslyn.Compilers.AssemblyResolver
IsSubmission              : False
PreviousSubmissionProjectId :
HasDocuments              : True
DocumentIds               : {C:\O'Reilly\examples\C#\BeaverMusic
                             C:\O'Reilly\examples\C#\BeaverMusic\
                             C:\O'Reilly\examples\C#\BeaverMusic\
                             C:\O'Reilly\examples\C#\BeaverMusic\
Documents                 : {Roslyn.Services.DocumentId, Roslyn.
```

The *BeaverMusic.sln* file is part of the examples available with this book. (Chapter 5 shows it in action.) Here, we use the Roslyn libraries to load the solution and loop through the Projects and then the DocumentIds, extracting the project name, $Project.DisplayName, and filename of each file in that project, Split-Path $Document.FileName -Leaf.

```
$slnFileName = "..\..\C#\BeaverMusic\BeaverMusic\BeaverMusic.sln"

$result = ForEach ($Project in
([Roslyn.Services.Solution]::Load($slnFileName)).Projects) {
    ForEach($Document in $Project.DocumentIds) {
        New-Object PSObject -Property @{
            ProjectName = $Project.DisplayName
            Filename    = Split-Path $Document.FileName -Leaf
        }
    }
}
```

```
$result | Format-Table -AutoSize
```

The results of running this script are as follows:

```
ProjectName          Filename
-----------          --------
BeaverMusic.UI.Shell AlbumEditDialogView.xaml.cs
BeaverMusic.UI.Shell AlbumEditDialogViewModel.cs
BeaverMusic.UI.Shell AlbumEditView.xaml.cs
BeaverMusic.UI.Shell AlbumEditViewModel.cs
BeaverMusic.UI.Shell AlbumListView.xaml.cs
BeaverMusic.UI.Shell AlbumListViewModel.cs
BeaverMusic.UI.Shell MainViewModel.cs
BeaverMusic.UI.Shell App.xaml.cs
BeaverMusic.UI.Shell MainWindow.xaml.cs
BeaverMusic.UI.Shell PowerShellConsoleLauncher.cs
BeaverMusic.UI.Shell AssemblyInfo.cs
BeaverMusic.UI       BindableBase.cs
BeaverMusic.UI       WatermarkTextBox.cs
BeaverMusic.UI       DelegateCommand.cs
BeaverMusic.UI       IViewFactory.cs
BeaverMusic.UI       AssemblyInfo.cs
BeaverMusic.UI       ViewElement.cs
BeaverMusic.UI       ViewFactory.cs
BeaverMusic          Album.cs
```

Rather than hardcode the $slnFilename, we could make it a parameter. It is as simple as this: param ($slnFilename). By doing this, we could use Get-ChildItem (aka dir or ls), find all the *.sln* files (passing each one to this script), and get a PowerShell array of objects with all of these details. Again, this is just a stepping-stone to composing a series of simple, targeted PowerShell functions to do a range of operations—from building targeted searches to generating reports or more code, just to name a few.

The properties on the Roslyn objects have insightful information. Also of interest are the methods we find on these objects.

Roslyn's Document Methods

The following script is slightly modified from the previous one. Here we want to take a look at what methods exist on the Documents property, which is found on the Project object. I've refactored this script to grab the first document in the first project using the –First parameter found on the Select cmdlet. I store that document in the variable $FirstDocument and pipe it to Get-Member, filter it for only methods (-MemberType Method), and sort the final result.

```
.\Add-RoslynLibraries

$slnFileName = Resolve-Path "..\..\C#\BeaverMusic\BeaverMusic.sln"

$FirstProject = ([Roslyn.Services.Solution]::Load($slnFileName)).Projects |
                Select -First 1
```

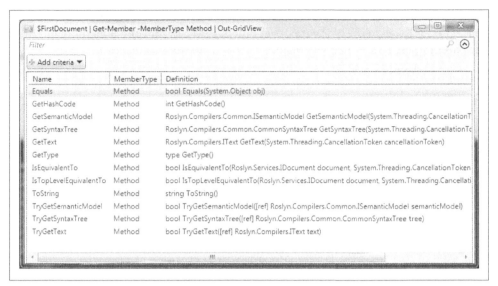

Figure 8-1. Piping Get-Member to Out-GridView

```
$FirstDocument = $FirstProject.Documents | Select -First 1

$FirstDocument | Get-Member -MemberType Method | Sort Name
```

There are a few more methods than these, but here are the interesting ones:

```
TypeName: Roslyn.Services.Document

Name                  MemberType  Definition
----                  ----------  ----------
GetSemanticModel      Method      Roslyn.Compilers.Common.ISemanticModel
GetSyntaxTree         Method      Roslyn.Compilers.Common.CommonSyntaxTree
GetText               Method      Roslyn.Compilers.IText GetText
```

As you pipe results down through the ForEach mechanism, you can also pipe what you have to Get-Member so you can inspect the attributes of the object that is being passed via the PowerShell pipeline. Here is a neat trick: after piping the object through to Get-Member, you can opt to see it in a GUI that can filter the details (rather than seeing it print to the console) by piping it to Out-GridView. This technique is super-useful when the target object has lots of attributes or when there is lots of text scrolling by in the console (see Figure 8-1 and the code that follows). This is a nonblocking operation.

```
$FirstDocument | Get-Member -MemberType Method | Out-GridView
```

Next, we want to call the GetSyntaxTree() method and then the Root property on it. Why? Because it looks interesting, and we'll be able to pull key aspects from our C# code later, like the using statements.

```
$cancelToken = New-Object System.Threading.CancellationToken
$FirstDocument.GetSyntaxTree($cancelToken).Root
```

Wait, where did the $cancelToken come from, and why? How did I know to pass a CancellationToken to the GetSyntaxTree() method? If you invoke a method and drop the parentheses, PowerShell will display the overload definitions for it.

```
$FirstDocument.GetSyntaxTree

OverloadDefinitions
-------------------
Roslyn.Compilers.Common.CommonSyntaxTree
GetSyntaxTree(System.Threading.CancellationToken cancellationToken)
```

Here are the details from the Root property on the $FirstDocument variable:

```
Externs         : {}
Usings          : {System, System.Collections.Generic, System.Linq, System.Text...}
Attributes      : {}
Members         : {BeaverMusic.UI.Shell
                  }
EndOfFileToken  :
Parent          :
Kind            : CompilationUnit
FullSpan        : [0..605)
Width           : 605
FullWidth       : 605
```

We can grab the Root of the syntax tree and pull out all the using statements from the C# code.

```
$cancelToken = New-Object System.Threading.CancellationToken
$Root = $FirstDocument.GetSyntaxTree($cancelToken).Root

$Root.Usings | Select name
```

Here are the results:

```
Name
----
System
System.Collections.Generic
System.Linq
System.Text
System.Windows
System.Windows.Controls
System.Windows.Data
System.Windows.Documents
System.Windows.Input
```

There are many other properties you can use to extract meaningful data from code. This is a big step up from using string pattern matching or regular expressions. This gets down to the syntactical, semantic level of the source code.

Plus, you can do it in a few lines of PowerShell, and Microsoft will be supporting the Roslyn libraries going forward. So, as the language evolves, you aren't maintaining parsers and the code that comes with them.

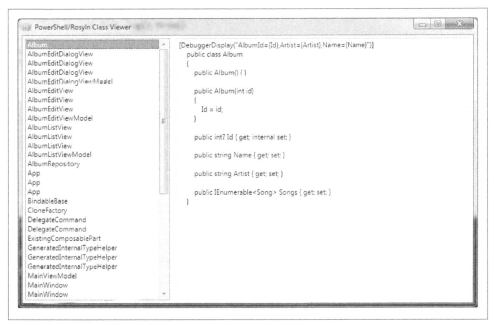

Figure 8-2. PowerShell Roslyn class viewer

PowerShell Roslyn Class Viewer

All this spelunking is nice—finding our way around .NET libraries (Roslyn, to be specific)—but now let's do something a bit more practical. I want to recursively search a directory of C# files (`*.cs`), look inside each, extract all the class names, and display them in a list box in a GUI. When I click on the class name in the list box, I want only the code defining that class to show up in a text box next to it on the righthand side (as shown in Figure 8-2).

You see repeated items for some classes because they are C# partial classes, and Roslyn returns them as such.

In Chapter 7, we walked through the ShowUI PowerShell module, which is designed to make creating WPF GUI applications easy in PowerShell.

 You can download ShowUI at *http://showui.codeplex.com/*.

If you run *ShowClasses.ps1* to import ShowUI, you'll get the class view of the sample C# application that accompanies this book. Clicking the class name on the left brings up the code on the right. This is very useful when you want to get a bird's-eye view of the general makeup of the files for a .NET application.

Plus, you don't need Visual Studio loaded up to get useful information about the C# code you're looking at.

How It Works at a High Level

ShowClasses.ps1 is where this kicks off; it calls *GetCSharpClass.ps1*, which calls upon *FindCSharpClass.ps1*, which in turn calls *InvokeRoslynCodeGen.ps1*. Here's a more detailed explanation of each script:

ShowClasses.ps1
> This script imports the ShowUI module, defines the layout of the GUI, and calls the `GetCSharpClass`, which retrieves all the information that is used to display the class names.

GetCSharpClass.ps1
> This script sets up the `New-Module` that is used to extract the class names and other details of the C# files. It "overrides" the `VisitClassDeclaration` method that Roslyn calls when it finds a class name.

FindCSharpClass.ps1
> This script is responsible for recursively searching directories for C# files (`*.cs`), passing them to the Roslyn `ParseCompilationUnit` (this returns the syntax tree), passing the PowerShell module created in `GetCSharpClass` to it, and returning the collected results.

InvokeRoslynCodeGen.ps1
> This cool script is modeled after the script in Chapter 4 that works with the abstract syntax tree for PowerShell code. Using PowerShell, it cracks open the `Roslyn.Com pilers.CSharp.SyntaxVisitor`, reflects over all the method signatures (including parameters), code-generates C# and then code-generates C# for each method, including a body of code to handle the invocation. At the end, it compiles the C# on the fly for use in the other PowerShell scripts.

Next, you'll find the *GetCSharpClass.ps1* script. Change the name of `VisitClassDecla ration` to match the name of one of the overridden `Visit*` methods in `Roslyn.Compil ers.CSharp.SyntaxVisitor`. You can find that in the Roslyn docs, or explore the DLL directly this way in PowerShell:

```
[Rosyln.Compilers.CSharp.SyntaxVisitor] |
    Get-Member Visit* -MemberType Method
```

For example, in `VisitFieldDeclaration`, the `$node` parameter will contain all the details about each of the field declarations found. Pull out the ones you are interested in and add them to the `$script:results` as `PSObjects` with properties.

Here is the *GetCSharpClass.ps1* script:

```
param (
    $targetDirectory
)
```

```
.\FindCSharpClass $targetDirectory (New-Module -AsCustomObject {

    $script:results = @()

    function VisitClassDeclaration ($node) {
        $script:results +=  New-Object PSObject -Property @{
            Name  = $node.Identifier.Value
            Class = $node.Identifier
        }
    }

    # Implicit interface
    function GetResults {
        $script:results
    }
})
```

Summary

Using PowerShell to glue together powerful components is a made-to-order scenario for scripting and .NET DLLs. The discovery process demonstrated in this chapter is one you can use over and over on .NET libraries you come across. The steps are:

1. Load the DLL in to the current PowerShell session.
2. Pipe .NET types or instances to Get-Member to discover the methods and properties you can access.
3. Rinse and repeat.

## CHAPTER 9

Writing Little Languages in PowerShell

The term *little language* was coined by Jon Bentley in a 1986 article he wrote for *Communications of the ACM* (*http://bit.ly/akBpXr*).[1] Little languages are also referred to as *domain-specific languages*, or DSLs.

Some little languages are intended to save development time and effort by allowing a developer to express his or her intentions at a much higher level of abstraction. This allows the developer's programs to be much shorter than equivalent programs in other languages. The "little" part primarily refers to the scope of what the language tackles.

In this chapter, we will focus on using PowerShell as a better XML, building our own little language that can do more than just plain XML. Then, we'll build another DSL to blend Graphviz, an open source graph visualization toolset, into the PowerShell ecosystem. This offers us a better way to manipulate abstractions when working with structural information like diagrams of abstract graphs and networks.

There are many examples of DSLs in the software industry—for example, MSBuild is a little language, to my way of thinking. While others may view MSBuild as a build system that reads a specific schema of XML as input, I see it as a domain-specific language in an XML format, specific to dealing with Visual Studio builds.

One of the challenges of using MSBuild with XML happens when we want to extend it. Adding a custom task to MSBuild requires dropping into C#, inheriting from some base classes, overriding methods, and extracting parameters from XML for the task you're implementing. V4 of MSBuild supports inline tasks based in XML. It's an interesting cognitive switch to use XML with CDATA sections and then add C# code.

---

1. Jon Bentley, "Little languages," *Communications of the ACM* 29, no. 8 (1986): 711–21.

psake (pronounced "sah-kay") is a build automation tool written in PowerShell by James Kovacs (*http://bit.ly/ACMUpZ*). It avoids the angle-bracket tax associated with executable XML by leveraging the PowerShell syntax in your build scripts. psake has a syntax inspired by rake (a.k.a. make in Ruby) and bake (a.k.a. make in Boo), but is easier to script because it leverages your existing command-line knowledge. You can download psake here: *http://bit.ly/tL8Hdz*.

Unlike MSBuild, extending psake is straightforward—you write more PowerShell.

Adding a New Construct to PowerShell

In PowerShell, it is simple to create a new construct. For example, here is a new looping construct:

```
function repeat {
    param (
        [int]$HowManyTimes,
        [scriptblock]$block
    )

    1..$HowManyTimes | Foreach { & $block }
}
```

Here we use that code to print "Hello World" three times:

```
PS C:\> repeat 3 {"Hello World"}

Hello World
Hello World
Hello World
```

Hat tip to Daniel Moore, who suggested a Ruby-style 3 | times {"Hello World"}.

This can be expressed as a filter—a function that just has a process script block. Plus, this one takes a script block as a parameter:

```
filter times ([Scriptblock]$Block) {
    1..$_ | ForEach { & $Block }
}

PS C:\> 3 | times {"Hello World"}
Hello World
Hello World
Hello World
```

Seeing PowerShell functions and script blocks used in this way opens the door to little languages. It is quick and inexpensive to put together a targeted little language from scratch. Other benefits to building a little language in PowerShell are PowerShell's approachability and the properties of an internal DSL. Because you're building an internal DSL in PowerShell using PowerShell (we're getting meta here), any expression you use must be a legal expression in PowerShell. This means that the little language you construct automatically benefits from all that is available in the PowerShell session in which it is running.

Let's start by comparing the XML approach, an *external DSL*, to a PowerShell approach, an *internal DSL*. An internal DSL is a language created inside another language. Put another way (borrowing Martin Fowler's definition), "internal DSLs are particular ways of using a host language to give the host language the feel of a particular language." External DSLs, on the other hand, "have their own custom syntax and you write a full parser to process them."[2] Many XML configurations have ended up as external DSLs.

PowerShell: A Better XML

XML is used in many places, such as HTML, configuration files, Visual Studio project definitions, WSDL, data interchange formats, and more. Working with XML in PowerShell is one of its sweet spots. To-do lists, web pages, insurance claims, and configuration files are just some examples of ways to use XML to represent information.

Here is a simple to-do list in XML:

```
$houseworkXml = @"
<todo name="housework">
    <todoItem priority="high">Clean the house.</todoItem>
    <todoItem priority="medium">Wash the dishes.</todoItem>
    <todoItem priority="medium">Buy more soap.</todoItem>
</todo>
"@
```

We'll convert it to an XMLDocument in PowerShell like so:

```
$housework = [xml]$houseworkXml
```

Finally, we use dot notation on the XML nodes, which prints out the results:

```
PS C:\> $housework.todo.todoItem

priority #text
-------- -----
high     Clean the house.
medium   Wash the dishes.
medium   Buy more soap.
```

Now that was simple! We could then pipe that line to the Where cmdlet and filter on, for example, only medium-priority items.

2. *http://martinfowler.com/bliki/DomainSpecificLanguage.html*

But Wait—There's More

Let's rework the XML into a PowerShell little language representation. Here is what we want it to look like:

```
New-ToDoList housework {
    New-ToDoItem high "Clean the house."    # <1>
    New-ToDoItem medium "Wash the dishes." .
    New-ToDoItem medium "Buy more soap."
}
```

This looks similar to the **repeat** construct we started with initially. There is a function name, New-ToDoList, and a parameter, housework, followed by a PowerShell script block.

Building the New-ToDoList function

We create a New-ToDoList function that takes two parameters. The first parameter is the name of the to-do list and the second is the script block.

```
function New-ToDoList {
    param(
        [string]$ToDoListName,
        [scriptblock]$ScriptBlock
    )
}
```

You can see at <1> another function called New-ToDoItem. Let's build that function now.

Building the New-ToDoItem function

Again, this is very easy, very straightforward. We create a function, New-ToDoItem, with two parameters, both of which are strings—the first takes a **Priority**, and the second is the **Task**.

```
function New-ToDoItem {
    param (
        [string]$Priority,
        [string]$Task
    )
}
```

Where to put this function?

PowerShell lets you define functions inside of other functions. We'll do this by putting the New-ToDoItem function inside the New-ToDoList function. For this example, it makes passing the script around easier, and we'll use this nested scope to our advantage.

PowerShell is very flexible when it comes to ad hoc development. The "whipupitude" factor is impressive (this term comes from Perl). We can whip up this little language, try it, tweak it, and then if we decide we want to formalize it, no problem. We can spin these functions off to separate files, or host them in a PowerShell module and take advantage of that organizational approach.

Here is one PowerShell function nested inside another. At this point, these functions do pretty much nothing more than define the scaffolding of our little language. Next, we'll invoke/execute the script block and then flesh out the body of the New-ToDoItem, which is responsible for emitting the results as an object with properties.

```
function New-ToDoList {
    param(
        [string]$ToDoListName,
        [scriptblock]$ScriptBlock
    )

    function New-ToDoItem {
        param (
            [string]$Priority,
            [string]$Task
        )
    }
}
```

Invoking the script block

Notice <Annotation 1> in the following example. The & is the PowerShell call operator. It executes what is in the script block, meaning it will execute each of the New-ToDoItem lines we started within the envisioned little language.

```
function New-ToDoList {
    param(
        [string]$ToDoListName,
        [scriptblock]$ScriptBlock
    )

    function New-ToDoItem {
        param (
            [string]$Priority,
            [string]$Task
        )
    }

    & $ScriptBlock                # <Annotation 1>
}
```

All but one piece of the mechanics are in place for the little language to work. New lists can be named and to-do item tasks can be created, prioritized, and associated with it.

Next we'll add the final piece that will capture and emit these details to the PowerShell pipeline.

The New-ToDoItem Body

We'll create a new `PSObject` on the fly and add three properties—the name of the to-do list, the priority, and the task:

```
New-Object PSObject -Property @{
    ToDoListName = $TodoListName
    Priority = $priority
    Task = $task
}
```

Now we'll string all of these snippets of script together to form the little language for creating to-do lists.

Putting It All Together

Here is the final little language—not even a page of code. Plus, notice how from within the embedded function, New-ToDoItem, we can access the $ToDoListName parameter on the New-ToDoList function. This is super-useful and really adds to the whipupitude factor.

```
function New-ToDoList {
    param(
        [string]$ToDoListName,
        [scriptblock]$ScriptBlock
    )

    function New-ToDoItem {
        param (
            [string]$Priority,
            [string]$Task
        )

        New-Object PSObject -Property @{
            ToDoListName = $ToDoListName
            Priority = $Priority
            Task = $Task
        }
    }

    & $ScriptBlock
}
```

The Little Language in Action

Here we go, running our little language:

```
New-ToDoList housework {
    New-ToDoItem high "Clean the house."
```

```
        New-ToDoItem medium "Wash the dishes."
        New-ToDoItem medium "Buy more soap."
    }
```

This code produces the following output and looks like the results we got from our XML approach. These are PowerShell objects with properties, so we can pipe them to any other PowerShell cmdlets. We can filter, sort, export, and more.

```
Priority ToDoListName Task
-------- ------------ ----
high     housework    Clean the house.
medium   housework    Wash the dishes.
medium   housework    Buy more soap.
```

Is It Worth Creating Your Own Little Language?

Without a doubt, building little languages in PowerShell is something you want in your toolbox. They are easy to build, try, and maintain. Here is the key reason—you can't do this with XML:

```
New-ToDoList housework {
    New-ToDoItem high "Clean the house."
    New-ToDoItem medium "Wash the dishes."
    New-ToDoItem medium "Buy more soap."

    "Buy Beer", "Get Pizza", "Purchase Microsoft Stock" |
        ForEach {
            New-ToDoItem high $_
        }
}
```

Remember, this is an internal DSL, and any expression you use must be a legal expression in PowerShell. That is not a constraint. You get to use the entire reach of PowerShell in the little language you just built.

```
Priority ToDoListName Task
-------- ------------ ----
high     housework    Clean the house.
medium   housework    Wash the dishes.
medium   housework    Buy more soap.
high     housework    Buy Beer
high     housework    Get Pizza
high     housework    Purchase Microsoft Stock
```

We created two functions that take a combined four parameters for our to-do little language. The key enabler is the script block, which can contain any valid PowerShell expression. The call operator & then "runs" the script block, executing all the Power-Shell within it.

I've used this to great effect on many projects, creating configuration languages, code transformers, and more. I often look to the Ruby and Python communities (and others) for how they approach these challenges. They have been doing it very effectively for many years.

Now we'll turn our attention to writing DSL around an existing DSL, Graphviz. By doing this, we'll be able to better interact with this visualization directly from PowerShell in a very natural and expressive way.

Graphviz

In this last example of building DSLs in PowerShell, we'll build out the PowerShell functions needed to create nodes and edges for a graph. Then I'll demonstrate how to use this functionality to create a simple Hello World example, a structural relationship by squaring numbers, and finally a more practical example of getting the running processes on my box and graphing the companies that own them.

Graphviz's dot language is an example of a DSL. Graph visualization is a way of representing structural information as diagrams of abstract graphs and networks. It has important applications in networking, bioinformatics, software engineering, database and web design, machine learning, and in visual interfaces for other technical domains.

If you want to play along in this section, download Graphviz here: *http://www.graphviz .org/Download.php.*

Graphviz "Hello World"

Here goes the obligatory "Hello World" GraphViz example. Remember, it is a DSL, so let's dissect what we have in the string. First up is the command `digraph`. `G` is the name of the graph, and `digraph` takes commands inside curly braces: `{Hello->World}`. Both `Hello` and `World` are nodes connected by an edge.

```
PS C:\> "digraph G {Hello->World}" | dot -Tpng -o .\hello.png
PS C:\> .\hello.png
```

The string `"digraph G {Hello->World}"` is piped to the *dot* application. dot is "hierarchical," or layered, drawings of directed graphs. This is the default tool to use if edges have directionality. dot aims edges in the same direction (top to bottom, or left to right) and then attempts to avoid edge crossings and reduce edge length.

Hello World Visual

dot has many parameters—the ones we're using are `-T` and `-o`. The `-T` parameter tells dot what type of output to generate, so in this case `-Tpng` indicates a PNG format (*http: //www.libpng.org/pub/png/*). The `-o` tells dot to generate a file and takes a filename.

The `{Hello->World}` representation says `Hello` and `World` are nodes, and `->` indicates that there's an edge between them with `Hello` as the source. You can see in Figure 9-1 that the arrow is drawn from `Hello` to `World`.

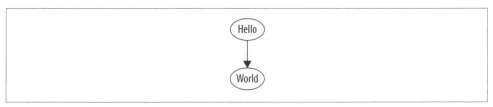

Figure 9-1. Hello World—Graphviz

A PowerShell DSL as a façade to GraphViz

GraphViz is already a terse and approachable little language, but we want to better enable it in the PowerShell environment. Here is how I'm envisioning we want to work with it, and then we'll build it:

```
New-Graph G {Add-Edge Hello World}
```

We want two functions, New-Graph and Add-Edge, in the *verb-noun* format so they're consistent with the rest of PowerShell. Add-Edge takes two parameters, source and target, for the nodes used in GraphViz. New-Graph takes two parameters, the name of the graph and a script block. The pattern is the same as the PowerShell to-do list DSL earlier in the chapter.

The PowerShell version is more verbose than GraphViz, but I'm okay with that because of what we'll be able to leverage later.

Building Add-Edge

Add-Edge is simple; it takes two parameters and creates a string from them with a -> between. We append that string to the variable $Script:edges. $Script: tells PowerShell to create the variable edges in the script scope. This is different than the $Global: scope. We'll create the variable edges next when we create the New-Graph function.

```
function Add-Edge {
    param(
        [string]$Source,
        [string]$Target
    )

    $Script:edges += "$Source->$Target"
}
```

Building New-Graph

New-Graph follows the same pattern as the New-ToDoList function in the first example of this chapter. The keys are the $ScriptBlock parameter and embedding the Add-Edge function in it.

We create the $Script:edges variable, set it to an empty array, @(), and then append to it each time an Add-Edge is called in the script block passed to the New-Graph.

```
function New-Graph  {
    param(
        [string]$Name,
        [scriptblock]$ScriptBlock
    )

    $Script:edges = @()

    function Add-Edge {
        param(
            [string]$Source,
            [string]$Target
        )

        $Script:edges += "$Source->$Target"
    }

    & $ScriptBlock

@"
digraph $name {
    $Script:edges
}
"@

}
```

Emitting output from New-Graph

New-Graph needs to generate the string "digraph G {Hello->World}". Adding the here-string, indicated by the @"..."@, after & $ScriptBlock will generate the syntax needed for GraphViz to process.

```
PS C:\> New-Graph G {Add-Edge Hello World}

digraph G {
    Hello->World
}
```

Mix and Match PowerShell and GraphViz

Our newly minted PowerShell functions generate what we did by hand at the start of this chapter. Now, we can specify the PowerShell DSL on the lefthand side of the pipe and continue to use dot on the righthand side. This creates the same visual as before:

```
PS C:\> New-Graph G {Add-Edge Hello World} | dot -Tpng -o .\hello.png
PS C:\> .\hello.png
```

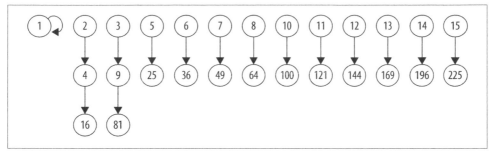

Figure 9-2. Graph squares of numbers

Kick It Up a Notch: New-Graph Is an Internal DSL

Remember, one of the great properties of an internal DSL is that any expression you use must be a legal expression in the host language. Since PowerShell is the host language, we get to use all of PowerShell when defining our graph.

Here, we're creating a range from 1 to 15, piping it to foreach, and creating an edge for that number to the square of that number.

You can't do this with the GraphViz DSL. While it takes some effort and cost to build the PowerShell wrapper, the benefits significantly outweigh the costs. Plus, the PowerShell implementation is 25 lines of code, much of which is plumbing (meaning defining the function and parameters calling the script block). It's less than a page of code.

```
New-Graph G {
    ForEach($x in 1..15) {
        Add-Edge $x ($x*$x)
    }
} | dot -Tpng -o .\test.png
```

What's interesting about tools like GraphViz that visualize graphs is that they'll do work for you. When we generate the edges from this simple algorithm, these two lines are produced (out of many more):

```
2->4
4->16
```

GraphViz recognizes this and "chains" the 2->4->16 in the resulting visual, as shown in Figure 9-2.

Graphing the Companies from Get-Process

In this final example, we tie together a real output using more of the PowerShell ecosystem in the New-Graph internal DSL.

Now I'm going to grab all the processes on my box, keeping only the ones where the Company property matches either Inc. or Corp. For each one found, we will create an

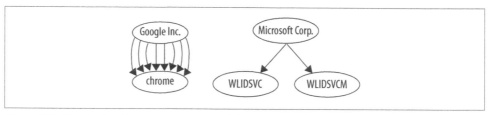

Figure 9-3. Graph of each process running and the company that owns it

edge between the `Company` and the `Name` of the process (see the resulting visual in Figure 9-3).

```
New-Graph G {

    Get-Process |
      Where {$_.Company -match 'Inc\.|Corp\.'} |
      ForEach {
          Add-Edge "$($_.Company)" "$($_.Name)"
      }

} | dot -Tpng -o .\test.png
```

You can't do this with GraphViz! By creating a simple DSL in PowerShell that transcodes these basics into the GraphViz DSL, we're unlocking some really cool possibilities.

Summary

Throughout this chapter, I've used the acronym DSL to describe our example, though some would call it a DSV (domain-specific vocabulary). Others suggest replacing these terms altogether with the definition of *library*. And it's true: building these types of solutions is similar to building libraries or frameworks. As Martin Fowler says in his book *Domain-Specific Languages* (Addison-Wesley Professional), "Indeed, most DSLs are merely a thinly veiled library or framework." Later, he describes the Ruby community's approach to library and framework design as a *more fluent approach*— that is, trying to make interacting with a library feel like programming in a specialized language.

Little languages, or DSLs, are good at taking slices of programming and making them easier to understand, easier to write, and quicker to modify, which can lead to fewer bugs.

Another benefit is that people with whom you collaborate and who need to read what you've written have a smaller surface to understand. The amount of ramp-up time required for learning a codebase can be a serious bottleneck. Learning the simple techniques shown in this chapter can help address that issue.

Look to the PowerShell community for many more examples of little languages. Simplifying complexity is one of PowerShell's key strengths, after all.

## CHAPTER 10

PowerShell, COM, and More

I bet almost every application you work with sports the option "Export to Excel." Good news: PowerShell too provides an easy path to interacting with Microsoft Office, via COM (Component Object Model). In this chapter, I'll show you how to "control" both Excel and Internet Explorer through a COM interface. Master this technique, and you'll find yourself leveraging it over and over. It provides quick solutions for your users, and soon you'll be using it in your day-to-day routines in ways you never expected.

Before I go down the COM route, I want to show you how you can use `Invoke-Item` to great effect.

Opening a File in Excel Using Invoke-Item

I have a file named *authors.csv*, the contents of which are shown in Figure 10-1. If I pass that filename to `Invoke-Item`, it will perform the default action for the file's extension on the specified item. Typing the following will launch Microsoft Excel and open *authors.csv*; see Figure 10-2.

```
PS C:\> Invoke-Item .\authors.csv
```

```
"Publisher","Title","Author","Year"
"CSLI","Literate Programming","Donald E. Knuth","1992"
"Addison-Wesley","More Programming Pearls","Jon Bentley","1990"
"Addison-Wesley","Compilers: Principles, Techniques, and Tools","Alfred V. Aho, et. al.","1986"
"Addison-Wesley","Patterns of Enterprise Application Architecture","Martin Fowler","2002"
```

Figure 10-1. Authors.csv file content

The `Invoke-Item` cmdlet is aliased to `ii`. Try the following:

```
PS C:\> ii .
```

This will launch the Windows file explorer in the current directory.

The return on investment (ROI) on these three characters is amazing.

⊿	A	B	C	D
1	Publisher	Title	Author	Year
2	CSLI	Literate Programming	Donald E. Knuth	1992
3	Addison-Wesley	More Programming Pearls	Jon Bentley	1990
4	Addison-Wesley	Compilers: Principles, Techniques, and Tools	Alfred V. Aho, et. al.	1986
5	Addison-Wesley	Patterns of Enterprise Application Architecture	Martin Fowler	2002

Figure 10-2. Launching Excel with Invoke-Item

On its own, using `Invoke-Item` at the command line is a gem. Next, we'll use it in a PowerShell script for an end-to-end solution.

Working Invoke-Item into a PowerShell Script

I'll work up some author data to illustrate this example. The important part is that the technique can be applied to any list created in PowerShell. This means you can query endpoints like SQL databases and web services, create arrays of PowerShell objects (lists), pipe them to an export cmdlet (like `Export-Csv`), and do an `Invoke-Item` on the resulting output file to display it in Excel—very cool and compelling.

Let's see an example to make things clearer. We'll create a `New-Author` function that transforms the four columns in our Excel sheet (Figure 10-2) into a PowerShell object with the column names as property names, and then set the values to those properties.

```
function New-Author {
    param (
        [string]$Author,
        [string]$Title,
        [string]$Publisher,
        [int]$Year
    )

    New-Object PSObject -Property @{
        Author    = $Author
        Title     = $Title
        Publisher = $Publisher
        Year      = $Year
    }
}
```

Now we'll use `New-Author` to create some author records:

```
New-Author "Donald E. Knuth" "Literate Programming" "CSLI" 1992
New-Author "Jon Bentley" "More Programming Pearls" "Addison-Wesley" 1990
```

We can capture the results to a variable using a PowerShell subexpression $().

```
$authors = $(
 New-Author "Donald E. Knuth" "Literate Programming" "CSLI" 1992
 New-Author "Jon Bentley" "More Programming Pearls" "Addison-Wesley" 1990
 )
```

The $authors variable contains a PowerShell list—an array of objects—with the appropriate author information. Piping this list to Export-Csv will convert the objects to comma-separated values and save it to a specified file. We're also specifying the -NoTypeInfomation switch because, by default, the first line of the CSV file contains #TYPE followed by the fully qualified name of the type of the object. The second line launches that file in Excel, as shown in Figure 10-2.

```
$authors | Export-Csv -NoTypeInformation .\authors.csv
Invoke-Item .\authors.csv
```

I use this approach a lot. Whatever data I have, I shape it, export it, and invoke it. Then, returning to the PowerShell script, I pull data from elsewhere, massage it, scrub it, filter it, add to or remove from it, and finally pipe and show it in Excel.

Many of these scripts are self-contained, so I can pass them around to colleagues or present them to my users, ready to run.

Let's continue working with Excel from PowerShell and see how we can tap into components you may not know about. Then, we'll look at how to control Excel through its COM interface.

Calling an Excel Function

Microsoft Excel is a powerful environment that makes it possible to analyze, manage, visualize, and share information. Microsoft has invested billions of research and development dollars over the years to make Excel what it is. It'd be unfortunate if we couldn't leverage this.

In the upcoming example, we're going to call four Excel functions, Median, StDev, Var, and Transpose. The first three are statistical functions that take an array and return a result. The last function, Transpose, returns a vertical range of cells as a horizontal range, or vice versa.

When you're working with Excel through the COM interface (or any application using COM), it is important to manage two things; the first is creating an Excel COM instance, and the second is releasing it. If you don't release the instance correctly, it will continue to run on your system.

Creating an Excel COM Instance

The New-Object cmdlet has a switch parameter, -ComObject. The ComObject parameter lets you specify the ProgID of a component you want to instantiate. In the case of Excel, its ProgID is Excel.Application.

Since we are interacting with Excel via COM, we need to play by COM rules, which means we need to do some housekeeping. We need to decrement reference count on the Excel object so that it can be freed. We do this by calling the ReleaseComObject()

method. We'll call this on both the `WorksheetFunction` object, `$wf`, and the Excel object, `$xl`, in that order.

```
$xl = New-Object -ComObject Excel.Application
$wf  = $xl.WorksheetFunction

$data  = 1,2,3,4
$array = ((1,2,3),(4,5,6),(7,8,9))

"Median   : {0}" -f $wf.Median($data)
"StDev    : {0}" -f $wf.StDev($data)
"Var      : {0}" -f $wf.Var($data)
"Transpose: {0}" -f ($wf.Transpose($array) | Out-String)

$xl.quit()

# Release the COM objects
$wf, $xl | ForEach {
    [void][Runtime.Interopservices.Marshal]::ReleaseComObject($_)
}
```

 In PowerShell, whether you're working with a PowerShell object, .NET object, or COM object, they are all treated the same. PowerShell is a great equalizer in this way.

Rerunning this script will instantiate and tear down an instance of Excel each time. Even though the data is mocked up for input, it could have easily come from files, databases, web services, and more.

Here we've simply output the results to the console. You can imagine scenarios where this data is collected, transformed, and sent to any number of destinations like other Excel sheets, other processes via REST, web services, or message queues.

```
Median   : 2.5
StDev    : 1.29099444873581
Var      : 1.66666666666667
Transpose: 1
4
7
2
5
8
3
6
9
```

Staying in alignment with one of PowerShell's core tenants, discoverability, let's see how we can discover what other Excel functions are available to use.

Discovering Available Excel Functions

How many Excel functions are there to choose from? The answer is 348!

Here is the GetExcelWorkfunction script. It has the familiar instantiation and teardown code for Excel. In the middle, we pipe the WorksheetFunction variable, $wf, to Get-Member. We want to see only the methods, so we use the -MemberType parameter and pass Method.

```
param($Name)

$xl = New-Object -ComObject Excel.Application
$wf  = $xl.WorksheetFunction
$wf |
    Get-Member -MemberType Method |
    Sort Name |
    Where {$_.Name -match $Name}

$xl.quit()

# Release the COM objects
$wf, $xl | ForEach {
    [void][Runtime.Interopservices.Marshal]::ReleaseComObject($_)
}
```

Here is how you use it:

```
PS C:\> .\GetExcelWorkfunction.ps1 | Measure-Object

Count    : 348
Average  :
Sum      :
Maximum  :
Minimum  :
Property :
```

GetExcelWorkfunction takes a parameter, $Name, so we can filter the method names more easily. For example, here are all the Excel worksheet functions that have the number 2 in them:

```
PS C:\> .\GetExcelWorkfunction.ps1 2

Name      MemberType Definition
----      ---------- ----------
Atan2     Method     double Atan2 (double, double)
Bin2Dec   Method     string Bin2Dec (Variant)
Bin2Hex   Method     string Bin2Hex (Variant, Variant)
Bin2Oct   Method     string Bin2Oct (Variant, Variant)
Dec2Bin   Method     string Dec2Bin (Variant, Variant)
Dec2Hex   Method     string Dec2Hex (Variant, Variant)
Dec2Oct   Method     string Dec2Oct (Variant, Variant)
Dummy21   Method     double Dummy21 (double, double)
Hex2Bin   Method     string Hex2Bin (Variant, Variant)
Hex2Dec   Method     string Hex2Dec (Variant)
Hex2Oct   Method     string Hex2Oct (Variant, Variant)
```

```
ImLog2     Method     string ImLog2 (Variant)
Oct2Bin    Method     string Oct2Bin (Variant, Variant)
Oct2Dec    Method     string Oct2Dec (Variant)
Oct2Hex    Method     string Oct2Hex (Variant, Variant)
SumX2MY2   Method     double SumX2MY2 (Variant, Variant)
SumX2PY2   Method     double SumX2PY2 (Variant, Variant)
SumXMY2    Method     double SumXMY2 (Variant, Variant)
T_Dist_2T Method      double T_Dist_2T (double, double)
T_Inv_2T  Method      double T_Inv_2T (double, double)
```

Calling More Excel Functions

Here I picked off a few decimal conversion methods from the previous list, and I also know there is a Factorial() method. Now let's call these.

```
$xl = New-Object -ComObject Excel.Application
$wf   = $xl.WorksheetFunction

"Dec2Bin   : {0}" -f $wf.Dec2Bin(2)
"Dec2Hex   : {0}" -f $wf.Dec2Hex(16)
"Dec2Oct   : {0}" -f $wf.Dec2Oct(8)
"Factorial : {0}" -f $wf.Fact(9)

$xl.quit()

# Release the COM objects
$wf, $xl | ForEach {
    [void][Runtime.Interopservices.Marshal]::ReleaseComObject($_)
}
```

Here are the results!

```
Dec2Bin   : 10
Dec2Hex   : 10
Dec2Oct   : 10
Factorial : 362880
```

This technique of instantiating a COM object and using Get-Member to display the methods available is not limited to Excel. On my Windows 7 Ultimate system, I have over 2,400 ProgIDs. This means I can instantiate and tap into over 2,400 different COM application objects in the same way I did Excel.

Keep reading to learn how to "control" Excel in PowerShell through its COM interface. I'll also show you how you can discover all the COM objects currently on your system.

Automating Excel from PowerShell

Learning to control Excel through its COM interface is extremely valuable. Here I'll show you how to launch Excel, create workbooks and worksheets, interact with cells, and create pivot tables—all from PowerShell. Then I'll provide a reusable function, Out-ExcelPivotTable, that can be applied in a variety of ways.

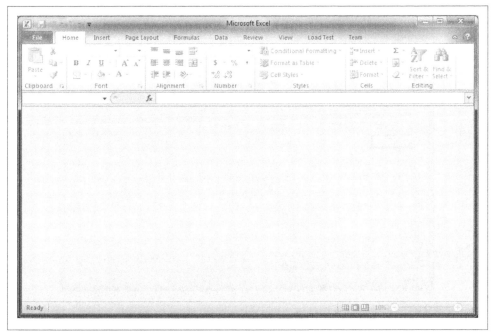

Figure 10-3. Making Excel visible

Using PowerShell to automate COM-enabled application is not limited to Excel.

```
(New-Object -ComObject Sapi.SpVoice).Speak("Hello PowerShell!")
```

Let's step through some of the basics to help you see how the pieces come together and also give you a sense of what you can do with other COM-enabled applications.

Making Excel Visible

Lifting the New-Object call in the previous examples, we can set the Visible property to true to launch Excel (see Figure 10-3).

```
$xl = New-Object -ComObject Excel.Application
$xl.Visible = $true
```

Notice that Excel is up and running, but doesn't have a workbook or worksheets. Let's fix that.

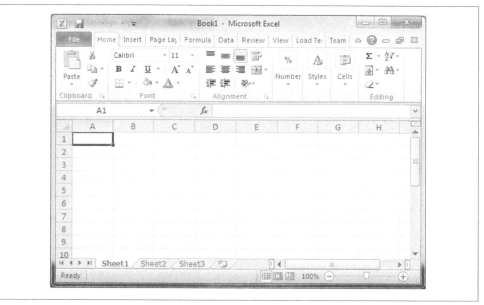

Figure 10-4. Create a workbook from PowerShell

Creating a Workbook and Worksheets

Creating a workbook or worksheet is easy! We'll add one line of PowerShell and call the Add() method on the Workbooks object to tell Excel to create a default workbook that has three worksheets defined (see Figure 10-4).

```
$xl = New-Object -ComObject Excel.Application
$xl.Visible = $true
$xl.Workbooks.Add() | Out-Null
```

Now, we'll populate Sheet1.

Putting the Date in a Cell in an Excel Worksheet from PowerShell

Working from the previous PowerShell script, we capture the new workbook in the $workbook variable, grab Sheet1 through the Item() method on the Worksheets object, and then access Cell A1 with the Item() method on the Cells collection. Here we set the cell value to the current date and time from PowerShell using the Get-Date cmdlet; see Figure 10-5.

The Excel model requires you to access it not by row column name A1, but rather by Row and Column numbers. This makes it easier to programmatically access cells directly.

```
$xl = New-Object -ComObject Excel.Application
$xl.Visible = $true

$workbook = $xl.Workbooks.Add()
```

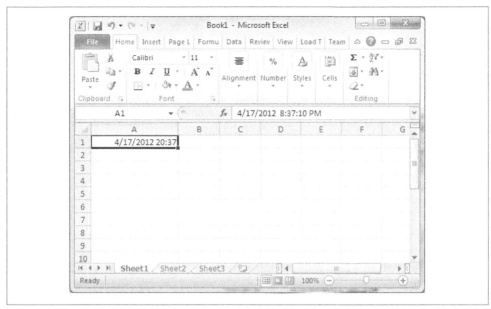

Figure 10-5. Date in cell from PowerShell

```
$sheet1 = $workbook.Worksheets.Item(1)
$sheet1.Cells.Item(1,1) = Get-Date
```

These five lines are a fundamental foundation for automating Excel from PowerShell. You can easily take any PowerShell collection, list, or array; loop through it and increment a row counter (and/or column counter); and place data into cells.

Next up, we'll do just that as well as cover how to call the `Create()` method on the `PivotCaches` object to display Excel pivot tables.

Setting Up Pivot Tables in Excel

In this final Excel example, we'll transform some raw data from a CSV file into an Excel pivot table. The data is a set of marketing and sales department professionals, their salary, and the number of years they have been employed. The first question we want to answer is how much the departments are being paid (see Figure 10-6).

We use the built-in PowerShell cmdlet to read the CSV file, which turns the data into objects with properties, and then pipe it to our script, specifying the properties we want to pivot on. This yields the results shown in Figure 10-6.

```
Import-Csv .\people.csv |
    .\Out-ExcelPivotTable.ps1 name dept salary
```

`Out-ExcelPivotTable` is worth reading, so get the scripts and take a look.

I'll highlight some snippets here. At its core, `Out-ExcelPivotTable` iterates over the data in the pipeline and lays it out in rows and columns in the spreadsheet. Along the way,

▲	A	B	C	D
1	Sum of Salary	Column Labels ▾		
2	Row Labels ▾	Marketing	Sales	Grand Total
3	Dawn		1400	1400
4	Dick	400		400
5	Harry	100		100
6	Jane		1100	1100
7	John	200		200
8	Tammy		1300	1300
9	Tina		1200	1200
10	Tom	300		300
11	Grand Total	1000	5000	6000

Figure 10-6. Marketing vs. sales

it captures the number of rows and columns, the names of the properties on the object, and their data types. The property names are used in the pivot table to set up both the Row Field and Column Field information. This creates the dimensions and measures for us to do analysis.

The data types of the properties are used to create smart defaults for the pivot table. If the data type is numeric, the defaults are set to Data Field (the measures); otherwise, they are set to Row Field or Column Field (the dimensions).

Building an Excel Pivot Table in PowerShell

Typically when I work with Excel, I'll turn on macro recording, click around the application to get what I want—in this case, a programmatic way to build Excel pivot tables—and then manually transcode the Visual Basic for Applications output into PowerShell. The variables $xlDatabase and $xlPivotTableVersion12 are constant values I defined in the PowerShell script.

```
$PivotTable = $Workbook.`
                PivotCaches().`
                 Create($xlDatabase,`
                   "Sheet2!R1C1:R$($rowCount)C$($columnCount)",`
                   $xlPivotTableVersion12
                 )
$PivotTable.CreatePivotTable("Sheet1!R1C1") | Out-Null
```

Here's the code filtering out numeric data types and creating the PivotFields with the orientation of Data Field (the measures):

```
$columns |
  Where { $_.definition -match "double|int|float"} |
    ForEach {
      $PivotFields = $Sheet1.`
        PivotTables("PivotTable1").`
        PivotFields($_.Name)
```

```
    $PivotFields.Orientation=$xlDataField
}
```

This feature of the script inspects the data type of the data for numbers, and then uses them as a Value in the pivot table; otherwise, it uses the data as a Row Label.

This illustrates the "principle of least surprise"—users can pipe some data to a function and get an Excel pivot table laid out in a usable format. Then, the users can think about it, type some more, pass parameters to Out-ExcelPivotTable, and get what they want: a differently shaped pivot table. Think a bit, type, and get what you want—that's what PowerShell delivers.

Now let's see how to leverage another core PowerShell principle—discovery.

Discovering Other COM Applications to Automate

Microsoft keeps a list of COM applications in the Windows Registry. PowerShell's Get-ChildItem cmdlet, aliased to dir and ls (for those UNIX grads), can easily access the Windows Registry. On my Windows 7 box, I can run this script (adapted from *http:// bit.ly/Jirftt*) and see that there are 2,400 COM applications registered.

```
param([string]$ProgId)

$paths = @("REGISTRY::HKEY_CLASSES_ROOT\CLSID")

if ($env:Processor_Architecture -eq "amd64") {
    $paths+="REGISTRY::HKEY_CLASSES_ROOT\Wow6432Node\CLSID"
}

Get-ChildItem $paths -Include VersionIndependentPROGID -Recurse |
    ForEach {
        New-Object PSObject -Property @{
            ProgId = $_.GetValue("")
            '32Bit' = & {
                if ($env:Processor_Architecture -eq "amd64") {
                    $_.PSPath.Contains("Wow6432Node")
                } else {
                    $true
                }
            }
        }
    } | Where {$_.ProgId -match $ProgId}
```

Now we can invoke it and count the number of ProgIds registered using the Measure-Object cmdlet.

```
PS C:\> .\GetProgID.ps1 | Measure

Count    : 2400
Average  :
Sum      :
Maximum  :
```

```
Minimum  :
Property :
```

Even Google has installed some COM applications.

```
PS C:\> .\GetProgID.ps1 google

ProgId
------
GoogleUpdate.Update3COMClassUser
GoogleUpdate.Update3WebUser
GoogleUpdate.OnDemandCOMClassUser
Google.OneClickProcessLauncherUser
GoogleUpdate.CredentialDialogUser
```

And here is a list of `ProgIds` that have either Excel or Word in them. Notice the fourth one down is the `ProgId` used in the examples in this chapter.

```
PS C:\> .\GetProgID.ps1 'excel|word'

ProgId
------
DTS.ConnectionManagerExcel
DTSAdapter.ExcelDestination
DTSAdapter.ExcelSource
Excel.Application
Excel.Chart
Excel.ChartApplication
Excel.OpenDocumentSpreadsheet
Excel.Sheet
Excel.SheetBinaryMacroEnabled
Excel.SheetMacroEnabled
IAS.ChangePassword
InfoPath.DesignerExcelImport
InfoPath.DesignerWordImport
OneNote.WordAddinTakeNotesButton
OneNote.WordAddinTakeNotesService
STSServer.EnumSTSWORDEDIT
VS10ExcelAdaptor
VS10WordAdaptor
Word.Application
Word.Basic
Word.Document
Word.DocumentMacroEnabled
Word.OpenDocumentText
Word.Picture
Word.Template
Word.TemplateMacroEnabled
```

There is a lot to discover in the Windows Registry where COM applications are concerned. You can Google for these `ProgIds`, see how others have used them, and then work up your own PowerShell solutions as an alternative.

Automating Internet Explorer as a COM Application

As a last example, we'll automate Microsoft Internet Explorer (IE) through its COM interface. Using GetProgID, we can search for the full ProgId based on a partial string. Then we can take the result and plug it into New-Object.

```
PS C:\> .\GetProgID.ps1 Explorer

ProgId
------
InternetExplorer.Application
```

After instantiating IE, we'll call the Navigate2() method and pass it the Bing URL. When you instantiate IE, it is not visible; you need to set the Visible property to $true.

```
$ie = New-Object -ComObject InternetExplorer.Application
$ie.Navigate2('http:\\www.bing.com')
$ie.Visible = $true
```

We could have launched the Bing search website another way: start *http://www.bing .com*. The difference is that start (the alias for Start-Process) launches the website in the default browser on your system. Using the COM automation approach, we ensure it launches in IE.

Last, from PowerShell we'll launch IE, navigate to Bing, turn off the address bar, go full screen, and show the browser.

```
$ie = New-Object -ComObject InternetExplorer.Application
$ie.Navigate2("bing.com")
$ie.AddressBar = $false
$ie.FullScreen = $true
$ie.Visible    = $true
```

Summary

We covered several key concepts in this chapter—for example, writing data to files with specific extension names and a comma-separated format, then launching Excel based on that extension name. Using COM automation, we reached in and worked with functions defined in Excel. Later, we wrote a script that discovered which Excel functions we could use. Finally, we automated workbooks and worksheets, placed data in specific cells, and created pivot tables, all through Excel's COM interface. Letting PowerShell be the glue between our data acquisition and data analysis, we learned how to discover what other COM applications exist on our system, then used that technique to find Microsoft Internet Explorer's COM name (ProgId) and automate that.

It's important here to point out the reach that PowerShell has. We were even able to tap into a decade-plus old technology, COM, from a 21st-century automation platform. That's pretty impressive, and it speaks to how much and how far Microsoft is investing in the PowerShell platform.

But there's still more to cover, so keep reading.

## CHAPTER 11

PowerShell Version 3

As of this writing, PowerShell v3 has been making its way to the public in the form of technology previews and with Microsoft Windows 8 and Windows Server 2012. The CTPs require Windows 7 Service Pack 1, Windows Server 2008 R2 Service Pack 1, and Windows Server 2008 Service Pack 2 (*http://bit.ly/KKXSBM*).

PowerShell v3 kicks things up a notch and is a multifront automation package. Windows Server 2012 delivers over 2,300 PowerShell cmdlets, up from 400. The product is better, faster, and more reliable; PowerShell has been refitted to use the Dynamic Language Runtime, or DLR (see *http://bit.ly/198u7X*).

 As Joel Bennett notes, because PowerShell 3 is based on the DLR, "scripts and functions are no longer (re)interpreted each time they're run; rather they are compiled, executed, and (sometimes) cached." For more details, see Joel's article here: *http://bit.ly/z4qwkB*.

PowerShell v3 also delivers on the client, adding more functionally across the board and making life easier to automate so we can do more business and add more value.

There is way too much to cover, so I'm going to pull out the PowerShell v3 pieces that I think highlight its benefits best. I (highly) recommend you install PowerShell v3, specifically Windows 8, and use this new version. PowerShell is not going away. Your investment in it not only makes you more productive, but it'll also help you rethink how to accomplish your daily tasks and write the components you deliver to clients.

PowerShell Workflows

First up is Windows *PowerShell Workflow* (PSWF). PSWF is the latest addition to the PowerShell family. A *workflow* is a set of activities that is stored as a model and depicts a process. The decision to integrate workflows into PowerShell starts with cloud computing and Windows-based datacenters.

Cloud computing provides a set of highly available, scalable computing services that leverage high-volume components (servers, disks, RAM, etc.). High-volume components are less reliable than their tier-one counterparts, and even those occasionally fail. The key to cloud computing management is to use software to deliver a reliable service in spite of failures. This is where workflows come in. Workflows are typically long-running scripts that are designed to survive component or network errors and reboots.

By automating tasks and operations, workflows decrease costs and improve repeatability, quality, auditing, and logging. This in turn allows you to take on more business and increase the value of your employees by freeing them up to deliver higher-quality functions.

PSWF allows developers to author sequences of activities that are:

- Long-running
- Repeatable
- Frequent
- Parallelizable
- Interruptible
- Suspendable
- Restartable

I'm going to dial into two ways you can author workflows. There are lots of resources on the Web that drill down on them, too. In addition, Microsoft will be making details available that analyze the new constructs in depth.

PowerShell Script-Based Workflow

PSWF is used to create applications that execute an ordered business process, such as the steps needed to approve a document, hire a candidate for a position, or make a purchase. These processes can execute in a short amount of time, but are typically long-running, in which case the application will need to shut down to conserve memory between steps.

Coupling workflow functionality with PowerShell lets you apply the benefits of workflows to the automation capabilities of PowerShell.

PSWF enables IT pros and developers alike to author sequences of multicomputer management activities—that are either long-running, repeatable, frequent, parallelizable, interruptible, stoppable, or restartable—as workflows.

As a demonstration, we'll create a workflow with four workflow activities. Three are WriteLine activities, and the fourth is a Delay activity. There is a new keyword, work flow. Like a function, it takes a name and a script block. This PowerShell script is transcoded into XAML workflow representation. The Start-Sleep is transcoded into a Delay workflow activity, and the other three into WriteLine workflow activities.

```
workflow Workflow1 {
    "Hello World"
    "Waiting 5 seconds..."
    Start-Sleep -Seconds 5
    "Goodbye"
}
```

Running the Workflow

We can run the workflow just like any other PowerShell function, as shown here. It looks and acts just like a normal function, but that is only the beginning.

```
PS C:\> Workflow1

Hello World
Waiting 5 seconds...
Goodbye

PS C:\>
```

We could also tack on the -AsJob switch, and this workflow would run as a background job. Again, this is only the beginning. Read on to see more.

Running the Workflow on Other Boxes

Using the workflow statement does a lot of work for you. It transcodes the PowerShell into XAML, code-generates a function, and adds a number of parameters to it. One of the parameters added is PSComputerName. This parameter lets you specify any number of boxes on which to run this workflow. Here we're specifying two boxes:

```
Workflow1 -PSComputerName finked-pc, finked-pc1
```

Discovering More About Your Workflow

We can use the PowerShell Get-Command to discover more about the workflow we created. As you know by now, discovery is a key tenant of PowerShell. Being able to drill deeper on objects and structures inside a PowerShell session is fundamental to helping you get your jobs done faster and with as little friction as possible. Workflows are no different.

```
PS C:\>Get-Command Workflow1

Capability Name        ModuleName
---------- ----        ----------
Workflow   Workflow1

PS C:\>Get-Command Workflow1 -Syntax

Workflow1 [<WorkflowCommonParameters>] [<CommonParameters>]
```

Let's take a look at the XAML that this code generated. The XML included here is only a snippet of 80+ lines of generated XAML:

```
PS C:\> (Get-Command Workflow1).XAMLDefinition.Workflow1

<ns1:WriteOutput>
    <ns1:WriteOutput.InputObject>
    <InArgument x:TypeArguments="ns4:PSObject[]">
        <ns2:PowerShellValue
        x:TypeArguments="ns4:PSObject[]"
        Expression="&quot;Hello World&quot;" />
    </InArgument>
    </ns1:WriteOutput.InputObject>
</ns1:WriteOutput>
```

One really nice thing here is that Microsoft has preserved your investment. It has introduced key workflow capabilities into PowerShell and has done so in such a way that you can use the same techniques you've been using since version 1.

Visual Studio Workflow

Now, we'll reproduce the same workflow as before using Microsoft Visual Studio and the Workflow Designer. This will produce a XAML file that we'll use directly in PowerShell using the Import-Module cmdlet. The upshot is that we can use any Workflow 4.0 XAML created, regardless of whether it was authored in PowerShell v3. The added benefit is that once the workflow is imported to PowerShell, it is part of the ecosystem. It's discoverable, composable, and remotable.

 While many of the PowerShell semantics are preserved, there are a number of breaks from how a PowerShell script operates with a workflow. Additionally, due to the conversion process, there are tricks to nesting workflows that are declared externally from each other (versus nested workflows). The semantics are different and beyond the scope of this book.

Furthermore, setting up a workflow in Visual Studio allows you to devise tests for the flow. And, as your workflow becomes more complicated, you have a visual representation of it, not just code. However, this is a double-edged sword. Using a designer with a complicated workflow can make it harder to navigate as compared to just code.

Figure 11-1. Windows workflow in the designer

We can use Visual Studio to create a new Workflow solution. We double-click the *Workflow1.xaml* file in the Solution Explorer (the same one that we discovered using `Get-Command`), drag out the `WriteLine` and `Delay` workflow activity components from the toolbox, and set up their properties (see Figure 11-1).

Once saved, the XAML file is ready to be imported.

Import-Module on a XAML workflow

I think you'll find this piece simple and straightforward, just like working with a PowerShell module:

```
PS C:\> Import-Module .\Workflow1.xaml
PS C:\> Workflow1
Hello World
Waiting 5 seconds...
Good bye
```

This authoring approach gets all the same benefits as a PowerShell script-based approach, including discoverability and the fact that it can be run on multiple boxes. If you have workflows that already exist, you can use them in PowerShell (WF v4.0) or you can work them up from scratch. Options are always good.

Getting performance counters in parallel

I often want to collect several Windows performance counters, so I use PowerShell's cmdlet Get-Counter. This cmdlet works off the same data as Perfmon. For example, here we'll retrieve the info for % Processor Time:

```
PS C:\> Get-Counter '\Processor(*)\% Processor Time'

3/17/2012 3:21:05 PM  \\finked-pc1\processor(0)\% processor time :
                      1.53800515935968

                      \\finked-pc1\processor(1)\% processor time :
                      4.61494249812969

                      \\finked-pc1\processor(2)\% processor time :
                      1.53800515935968

                      \\finked-pc1\processor(3)\% processor time :
                      3.07647382874469

                      \\finked-pc1\processor(_total)\% processor time :
                      2.69184926496185
```

Moving on to collect multiple counters, we could simply create an array of performance counter strings and foreach over them, passing them to Get-Counter. That would execute them sequentially, though.

With two tweaks, we can use foreach and make this happen. First, we'll wrap it in a workflow, and then we'll use the new -parallel construct on the foreach statement. The -parallel for the foreach can be used only inside a workflow.

```
workflow Invoke-PerfCounter {
    param($counters)

    foreach -parallel ($counter in $counters)
    {
        (Get-Counter $counter).CounterSamples |
            Select -Property Path, CookedValue
    }
}

$counters = '\Processor(*)\% Processor Time',
    '\Processor(*)\% User Time',
    '\Process(*)\Handle Count',
    '\Process(*)\IO Read Operations/sec',
    '\Process(*)\IO Write Operations/sec',
    '\Process(*)\IO Data Operations/sec'

Invoke-PerfCounter $counters
```

That's it—we're collecting and displaying performance data in parallel.

This is another advantage of using workflows in PowerShell: you can parallelize your work.

Why workflows rock

PSWF is a flagship feature in v3. It is a tremendous addition to the ecosystem, and I expect third-party vendors will both leverage it and provide tools to create some serious timesaving implementations.

Scripting a workflow has many benefits, and a key one is that we can do it all in PowerShell. This means when we hit a wall, we have the opportunity to work up some more PowerShell to integrate workflow with other components or subsystems in the Windows environment.

 At the beginning of the chapter, I listed bullet points for *interruptible*, *suspendable*, and *resumable*. I have not shown any examples of these features because it would take entire chapters to treat that material appropriately. Keep an eye on the community blogs and the PowerShell team blog for exciting details on these as well as the new constructs.

For an excellent drill-down, check out this video of Bruce Payette on PowerShell Workflows: *http://bit.ly/AvoCaS*.

Using PowerShell with Web Data: Converting to and from JSON

JavaScript Object Notation (JSON) is a lightweight, text-based open standard designed for data interchange. Despite its relationship to JavaScript, it is language-independent, with parsers available for many languages, including PowerShell.

The JSON format is often used for serializing and transmitting structured data over a network connection. It is used primarily to transmit data between a server and web application, serving as an alternative to XML.

The following example shows the JSON representation of an object that describes a person. The object has string fields for first name and last name, has a number field for age, contains an object representing the person's address, and contains a list (an array) of phone number objects.

```
$json = @"
{
    "firstName": "John",
    "lastName" : "Smith",
    "age"      : 25,
    "address"  :
    {
        "streetAddress": "21 2nd Street",
        "city"         : "New York",
        "state"        : "NY",
        "postalCode"   : "10021"
    },
    "phoneNumber":
    [
        {
```

```
            "type"   : "home",
            "number": "212 555-1234"
        },
        {
            "type"   : "fax",
            "number": "646 555-4567"
        }
    ]
}
"@
```

Converting JSON to PowerShell Objects and Back Again

There's a one-liner to take a string of JSON and convert it to a PowerShell representation. The variable $PowerShellRepresentation contains the object, complete with properties and nested structures:

```
PS C:\> $PowerShellRepresentation = $json | ConvertFrom-Json
```

Now, let's access the string we converted in PowerShell:

```
PS C:\> $PowerShellRepresentation

firstName    : John
lastName     : Smith
age          : 25
address      :
  @{streetAddress=21 2nd Street; city=New York; state=NY; postalCode=10021}
phoneNumber  :
  {@{type=home; number=212 555-1234}, @{type=fax; number=646 555-4567}}
```

Now we'll pick off the address:

```
$PowerShellRepresentation.address


streetAddress city      state postalCode
------------- ----      ----- ----------
21 2nd Street New York NY     10021
```

Finally, we'll grab the phone numbers:

```
$PowerShellRepresentation.phoneNumber

type number
---- ------
home 212 555-1234
fax  646 555-4567
```

PowerShell can interoperate with JSON, which is a lighter weight XML. Being able to consume text and turn it into objects with properties makes it super-easy to get at information and consume it in the way you need to.

This isn't a one-way ticket, though; we can take the round-trip. We'll take the JSON we converted to PowerShell and pipe it to `ConvertTo-Json`, and it will produce the JSON string we started with originally.

```
$PowerShellRepresentation | ConvertTo-Json
```

This means we can work in PowerShell, doing directory listings (PowerShell objects), reading XML (PowerShell objects), calling methods on .NET DLLs, getting results (PowerShell objects), and more. Then, we can pipe results to `Convert-ToJson`, and we're ready to interact with services that accept JSON.

What If a Web/REST Service Returns JSON?

If JSON is returned by a web or *representational state transfer* (REST) service, no problem—PowerShell has a cmdlet that makes it incredibly easy to handle the request and conversion all in a couple of lines of script:

```
$url = 'http://search.twitter.com/search.json?q=powershell'
(Invoke-RestMethod $url).results
```

Or even less if we use an alias:

```
(irm $url).results
```

Here is the first element of the array returned from the Twitter search we just ran. Remember, each is accessible via the property name. Plus, because we are working with PowerShell, we can leverage PowerShell's other cmdlets, like `Export-Csv`, and pipe the results to a comma-separated value file. This preps it for use in Excel, for example. That's a great return on a single line of code.

```
created_at              : Sat, 24 Mar 2012 16:54:47 +0000
from_user               : denisemc06
from_user_id            : 78444415
from_user_id_str        : 78444415
from_user_name          : Denise McInerney
geo                     :
id                      : 183597742919135233
id_str                  : 183597742919135233
iso_language_code       : en
metadata                : @{result_type=recent}
profile_image_url       : http://a0.twimg.com/profile_images/1637362430/
headshot3_small_normal.jpg
profile_image_url_https : https://si0.twimg.com/profile_images/1637362430/
headshot3_small_normal.jpg
source                  : &lt;a href=&quot;http://www.tweetdeck.com&quot;
rel=&quot;nofollow&quot;&gt;TweetDeck&lt;/a&gt;
text                    : Getting #powershell schooling from @SQLvariant at #sqlsat120
to_user                 :
to_user_id              :
to_user_id_str          :
to_user_name            :
```

So, we can now consume and produce JSON, the Internet *lingua franca*. We can query REST services and let PowerShell automatically convert JSON to PowerShell objects, which can be piped to other PowerShell functions/cmdlets and transformed to different shapes and formats. Anytime I find myself reaching for cUrl or wget, I first check if I can do what I need in PowerShell v3.

Creating an Instance of a Microsoft .NET Framework Object

There is a welcome improvement to the PowerShell v3 toolbox: PSCustomObject. In typical PowerShell fashion (which shows Microsoft is listening), PSCustomObject reduces the amount of code you produce and improves results.

In previous versions of PowerShell, you'd use the New-Object cmdlet, passing it a Type Name of PSObject, and a hash table to create an object with properties.

```
New-Object PSObject -Property @{
    FirstName = "Donald"
    LastName  = "Knuth"
}
```

An unwanted side effect of this approach was that you needed additional code to get the properties to appear in the order you wanted:

```
LastName FirstName
-------- ---------
Knuth    Donald
```

PSCustomObject handles this, and in less code:

```
[PSCustomObject] @{
    FirstName = "Donald"
    LastName  = "Knuth"
}
```

PSCustomObject is now the preferred way to create a new object and add properties:

```
FirstName LastName
--------- --------
Donald    Knuth
```

While we're on this subject, I want to point out that PowerShell v3 lets you create objects by passing a hash table with their property values. This is similar to object and collection initializers in C#.

```
Add-Type -TypeDefinition @"
namespace Example {
    public class Test {
        public string FirstName {get; set;}
        public string LastName {get; set;}
    }
}
"@

[Example.Test] @{
```

```
        FirstName = "Donald"
        LastName  = "Knuth"
}
```

This is a very handy way to work with .NET and creating objects, as you can see from the following outcome:

```
FirstName LastName
--------- --------
Donald    Knuth
```

 If you want to create an object with a known type, the type must have a default constructor—that is, one with no parameters.

Get-Content –Tail

Before PowerShell v3, you could not easily *tail* a file using PowerShell. Tail is a program on UNIX and UNIX-like systems used to display the last few lines of a text file or piped data (*http://en.wikipedia.org/wiki/Tail_(Unix)*).

This is very handy to use when you're looking at a logfile that is being written to. To quickly simulate this, launch PowerShell. Type **notepad test.txt** and press Enter. Notepad will prompt you to create a new file if necessary. Enter a few lines of data, like 1, 2, 3, on separate lines, and save the file. Switch back to the PowerShell console and type this:

```
Get-Content .\test.txt -Wait -Tail 1
```

Get-Content reads the contents of a file. The –Wait parameter waits for contents to be appended to the file. The –Tail parameter indicates how many lines from the end of the file are read.

So, to summarize, firing up that line of code in the console will make it sit there and spit out the last line of the target file every time it is updated.

ISE v3

The PowerShell team has been hard at work improving the Integrated Scripting Environment (ISE). Just type **ise** at the PowerShell command line, and you're in. ISE is part of the PowerShell v2/v3 install (Figure 11-2). It uses the Visual Studio edit control and supports a similar workflow to Visual Studio itself. Type some code in the script pane and press F5; it runs the script, showing the results in the console pane. In addition, ISE v3 supports syntax highlighting and debugging.

```
1  function Test {
2      if( get-com
3  }
```

Figure 11-2. PowerShell ISE v3 code folding and IntelliSense

On Server operating systems, ISE is an optional feature and it cannot be used on the Server Core installation option.

Pressing F9 toggles a debug breakpoint; press F5 to run the script, and ISE will break at that line. You can hover over variables to see their value, and you are in a suspended PowerShell session. Drop down to the console pane, and you can type out variables and inspect the current state of the session.

PowerShell ISE v3 brings many other new features, like code folding, snippets, and IntelliSense, at several levels. As you type cmdlets or functions, the drop-down filters the list. In addition, when you type a hyphen (-) for a parameter, context-sensitive IntelliSense presents a list of parameters for just that cmdlet or function.

When working on scripts longer than a single line, you'll find ISE v3 is a valuable tool for sifting through code and debugging problems.

If you are comfortable editing code in Visual Studio, you'll be right at home with ISE v3.

Out-GridView and the -PassThru Parameter

Out-GridView is such a handy tool—think of it as injecting a GUI into your command line. Considering it this way can lead you toward building very powerful components.

In PowerShell v3, Out-GridView got a new parameter, -PassThru (Figure 11-3). When specified, -PassThru sends the selected items from the interactive window down the pipeline as input to other commands.

Out-GridView also has a parameter, -OutputMode, which can take one of three values: None | Single | Multiple. Choosing Multiple is the same as using –PassThru.

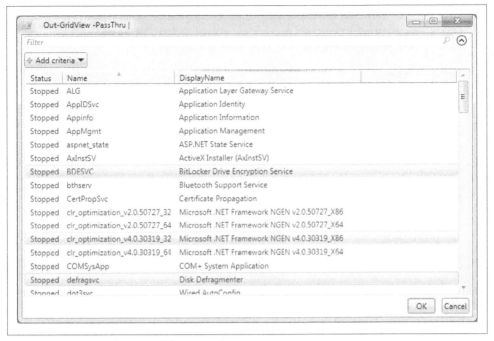

Figure 11-3. Out-GridView and the –PassThru parameter

Here we want to view all the stopped services in Out-GridView. Plus, we want to be able to select one or more of the services, and when we click OK, those services—and only those services—will start.

```
Get-Service |
    Where Status -eq Stopped |
    Out-GridView -PassThru |
    Start-Service
```

If none is selected or the Cancel button is clicked, no services are sent down the pipeline and nothing happens.

We wrapped that previous snippet in a function, Show-StoppedService. How many others can you think of to wrap like this and make life simpler?

```
function Show-StoppedService {
    Get-Service |
        Where Status -eq Stopped |
        Out-GridView -PassThru |
        Start-Service
}
```

Scheduling Jobs

PowerShell's scheduled jobs are a useful hybrid of PowerShell background jobs and Windows Task Scheduler tasks. (See more info at *http://bit.ly/H5AoYW*.)

Let's see what commands are exported from the PSScheduleJob module:

```
PS C:\> Import-Module PSScheduledJob
PS C:\> (Get-Module PSScheduledJob).ExportedCommands.Keys

Add-JobTrigger
Disable-JobTrigger
Disable-ScheduledJob
Enable-JobTrigger
Enable-ScheduledJob
Get-JobTrigger
Get-ScheduledJob
Get-ScheduledJobOption
New-JobTrigger
New-ScheduledJobOption
Register-ScheduledJob
Remove-JobTrigger
Set-JobTrigger
Set-ScheduledJob
Set-ScheduledJobOption
Unregister-ScheduledJob
```

Scheduled jobs have a ton of capability, like triggering when the battery status changes, when the network is connected, when the system is idle, and much more. Keep an eye out for lots of functionality from the PowerShell community in this area.

There are three steps to working with a scheduled job: create a trigger `New-JobTrigger`, register it with `Register-ScheduledJob`, and after it has run, retrieve its results with `Get-Job | Receive-Job`.

 If not in the same PowerShell session where the commands were invoked, you'll need to import the PSScheduledJob module so that you can read the status of PowerShell scheduled jobs.

Now, I want to combine steps one and two as an example and show how you can compose your own solutions to make scheduling a task simple.

Let's say we want to run a job one time five seconds from now to get the services running on our system. Here is what we'd like to type at the console:

```
Start-ScheduledJobIn TestGetService 5 {Get-Service}
```

Here's the `Start-ScheduledJobIn` function:

```
function Start-ScheduledJobIn {
    param (
        [string]$Name,
        [int]$SecondsFromNow,
        [ScriptBlock]$ScriptBlock
    )

    $trigger = New-JobTrigger `
        -Once `
```

```
        -At (Get-Date).AddSeconds($SecondsFromNow)

    Register-ScheduledJob `
        -Name $Name `
        -ScriptBlock $ScriptBlock `
        -Trigger $trigger
}
```

We can expand this function in many ways, but it is important to note that:

- You need to run `Unregister-ScheduledJob` to remove the scheduled job.
- You need to use `Get-Job TestGetService | Receive-Job` to see the results of its execution.

These few commands help you get familiar with scheduled jobs so you can work with them. Since it is all PowerShell-based, customizing solutions for specific scenarios is simple and plays to PowerShell's scenario-based development.

Invoke-WebRequest and Invoke-RestMethod

`Invoke-WebRequest` and `Invoke-RestMethod` are two new cmdlets that make working with the Web easier. They are used for two different endpoints.

`Invoke-WebRequest` is great because it parses the response, exposing collections of forms, links, images, and other significant HTML elements.

This next snippet retrieves a chunk of PowerShell from the URL, which is then evaluated with `Invoke-Expression`. The `Invoke-Expression` cmdlet evaluates or runs a specified string as a command and returns the results of the expression or command. I suggest you run it to experience it.

```
Invoke-Expression (Invoke-WebRequest http://bit.ly/eOMw9w).Content
```

In the final release of PowerShell v3, it may be possible to use fewer characters as follows. Here we're using the aliases of the two cmdlets and dropping the .Content.

```
iex(iwr http://bit.ly/eOMw9w)
```

`Invoke-RestMethod` can make requests to REST-compliant ("RESTful") web services. It returns HTML responses as HTML documents and JSON responses as JSON objects.

One of `Invoke-RestMethod`'s parameters is –ReturnType, which can be set to Detect, Json, or XML. The default is Detect. This lets you retrieve and output an XML RSS feed in one line of PowerShell, compared to three lines of PowerShell in v2. That's a 66% savings.

```
Invoke-RestMethod http://goo.gl/ZC76L | Select Title, PubDate
```

Here are the results of the `Invoke-RestMethod` line of code in XML, neatly packaged as PowerShell objects with properties:

```
title                                             pubDate
-----                                             -------
I'll be Judging the PowerShell 2012 Scripting Games   Mon, 12 Mar
Using PowerShell v3 to consume the StackOverflow JS...  Thu, 09 Feb
PowerShell Script to List the Organizations Support...  Sat, 21 Jan
Using PowerShell to solve Project Euler: Problem 1    Sun, 08 Jan
PowerShell and IEnumerable<T>                         Sat, 24 Dec
PowerShell, Windows Azure and Node.js                 Sat, 17 Dec
How to find the second to last Friday in December-U...  Sat, 17 Dec
PowerShell - Using the New York Times Semantic Web ...  Sun, 04 Dec
My First PowerShell V3 ISE Add-on                     Sun, 04 Dec
Use PowerShell V3 to Find Out About Your Twitter Fo...  Thu, 24 Nov
```

You could also slice and dice Twitter search results for PowerShell tweets:

```
(Invoke-RestMethod http://goo.gl/Vdyji).results |
    Select from_user, created_at, text
```

The same cmdlet is used for the RSS feed retrieval; this time, JSON was returned and parsed to create PowerShell objects with properties:

```
from_user       created_at  text
---------       ----------  ----
mariettol       Sun, 18 Mar Check out Microsoft Script Explorer f
PSdownunder     Sun, 18 Mar If you're having trouble getting to t
clintonskitson  Sun, 18 Mar RT @jsnover: When Windows PowerShell
chrisbrownie    Sun, 18 Mar The #psdu web site is struggling a li
Clarkezone      Sun, 18 Mar Windows Azure PowerShell Cmdlets http
mwjcomputing    Sun, 18 Mar RT @proxb: 2012 Scripting Games start
Cliff__Davies   Sun, 18 Mar Check out this article on http://t.co
ihunger         Sun, 18 Mar #PowerShell Use PowerShell to Find an
KzSundaySilence Sun, 18 Mar RT @JeffHicks: Video: Bruce Payette -
JeffHicks       Sun, 18 Mar Video: @jamesoneill shares his #Power
proxb           Sun, 18 Mar 2012 Scripting Games start 2 weeks fr
TCEJobs         Sun, 18 Mar Build Engineer - Powershell - Documen
mrpjscott       Sun, 18 Mar RT @PSdownunder: Released today: Our
ATLPUG          Sun, 18 Mar [ATLPUG] International PowerShell Use
AllEngineerJobs Sun, 18 Mar Build Engineer - Powershell - Documen
```

PowerShell v3 Items That Are a Must-See

PowerShell v3 brings numerous updates to the table in the form of fixes, additions, performance improvements, and more reliability. Other improvements are better discoverability and syntax simplification.

Show-Command

When you launch PowerShell, you are looking at a blank screen. That's a tough way to get started if you haven't spent time within the environment. With PowerShell v3, you can type Show-Command and press Enter. You will be presented with a dialog, as shown in Figure 11-4. From here, you can filter the list either by using the drop-down to select a PowerShell module, typing a command in the text box, or selecting a

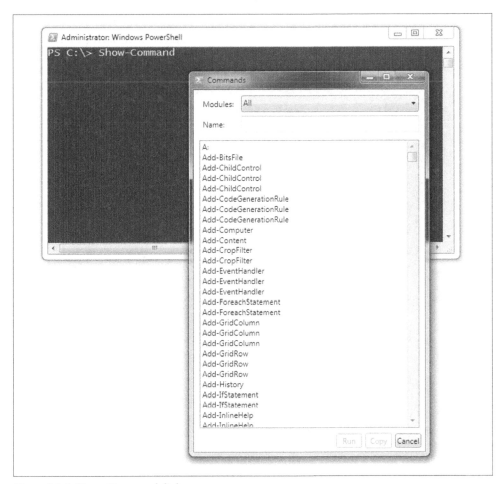

Figure 11-4. Show-Command dialog

command in the list box. Once you've selected a function/cmdlet, you can begin to drill down into the details of that selection. You'll be presented with the parameters that the command supports, and you can provide values for them in the dialog itself.

From there, you can run the command directly by clicking the run button or copy it to the clipboard by clicking copy. In other words, you can copy and paste the correctly formed PowerShell line, complete with parameters and values. Another nice feature of the dialog is that if a parameter is an enumeration, it shows up in a drop-down list.

Show-Command also lets you specify a function or cmdlet as a parameter. It shortcuts your searching for it (see Figure 11-5).

```
Show-Command Get-Command
```

Finally, Show-Command can be docked in the ISE. You can toggle this using the View menu (see Figure 11-6).

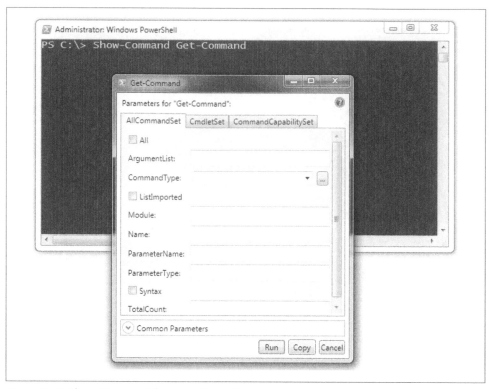

Figure 11-5. Show-Command for a specific cmdlet

Figure 11-6. Enabling Show-Command in ISE

In Figure 11-7, you can see that the Show Command dialog is docked and ready. Note the context change of the button. After finding and setting the parameters of your command, you can select the Insert button to insert the final result into the console pane, ready for execution.

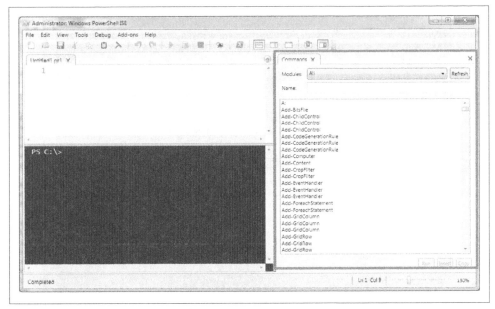

Figure 11-7. Show-Command docked in ISE

Less Typing for ForEach and Where

In PowerShell v3, Microsoft introduces a simplified syntax for the `Where` and `ForEach` cmdlets. The `$_` (current object automatic variable), braces `{}`, and dot operators are no longer required for simple constructs. Here is a `Where-Object` example:

```
Get-Process | Where Handles -gt 700
```

Compare this to the old version:

```
Get-Process | Where {$_.Handles -gt 700}
```

 This is for simple, single comparisons only. Complex evaluations are not supported.

Execute PowerShell Commands from the Web

Windows PowerShell Web Access lets you manage your Windows machines anywhere and anytime. (For more information, check out this blog post: *http://bit.ly/ykVTOl*.)

PowerShell Web Access is an Internet information services (IIS) web application that provides a PowerShell console in a web browser. The IIS application acts as a gateway from which you can connect to any machine in your environment that has PowerShell remoting enabled. Figure 11-8 shows a PowerShell console loaded up in a browser.

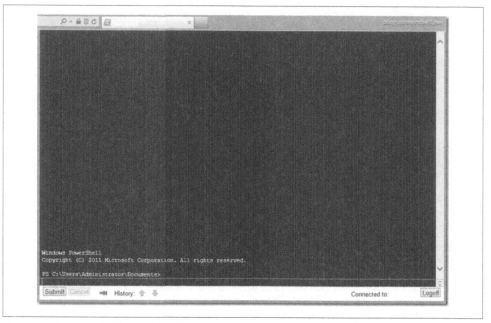

Figure 11-8. PowerShell console loaded up in a browser

Windows PowerShell Management ODATA IIS Extensions

Management ODATA IIS extensions enable a PowerShell scripter to expose a set of PowerShell cmdlets as a RESTful web endpoint accessible via the open data protocol (ODATA). This provides remote access to invoke cmdlets from both Windows and non-Windows clients. Check out the Management ODATA web services dev tools at *http://bit.ly/GPvin8*.

Management ODATA is an infrastructure for creating an ASP.NET web service endpoint that exposes your management data, accessed through PowerShell cmdlets and scripts, as ODATA web service entities. It does that by processing ODATA requests and converting them into a PowerShell invocation.

Product teams will build on top of this infrastructure to create endpoints that expose specific sets of management data.

Summary

Gartner, Inc. is the world's leading information technology research and advisory company, and one of the services it provides is forward-looking analysis. One of Gartner's predictions back in 2011 was that "tools and automation will eliminate 25% of labor hours associated with IT services" (*http://bit.ly/h5l06S*).

In this spirit, and as this chapter has outlined, we as developers can use PowerShell and these new v3 additions to enable automation:

- Streamlining activities
- Improving repeatability
- Improving quality
- Improving turnaround time

In the end, we can reclaim that 25%—or 10 hours in a 40-hour period—to do real problem solving.

Productive PowerShell

I recently saw a tweet saying, "If you repeat it, PowerShell it." I couldn't agree more.

In this appendix, I want to share a spectrum of examples to illustrate PowerShell's reach and primarily, to demonstrate that learning and using PowerShell in your day-to-day tasks will save you time. It's easy to sit back and think, "It's just a simple scripting language; I don't have time to invest in another technology that may not pan out," or "It'll take longer to automate than it will to just do it, and there are only a few steps to this, so I'll knock it out."

PowerShell's depth and reach is more than you can imagine, and growing every day. Plus, it is dynamic and powerful enough that if either Microsoft or the PowerShell community hasn't delivered a solution, PowerShell itself can take you the last mile.

 Automation is quickly moving from a "nice to have" feature to critical for delivering software in an ever-changing landscape.

Here, I'll present some places where developers choose not to automate, and I'll provide some PowerShell automation alternatives. In addition, one of the great perks of being a PowerShell MVP is being in the company of outstanding PowerShell MVPs (Table A-1). This is a group of passionate, smart people who are leveraging PowerShell in so many creative ways. Luckily for us, they are also generous—they have shared ideas and PowerShell snippets for me to include here.

Table A-1. PowerShell scripters and MVPs

Scripter	URL
Joel Bennett	*http://bit.ly/H0FiFA*
Keith Hill	*http://bit.ly/H45PRm*
Karl Prosser	*http://bit.ly/Hv3YsM*
Daniel Moore	*http://bit.ly/HeYsHV*

Scripter	URL
Aleksandar Nikolic´	http://bit.ly/H6ZFB7

Getting Automation Approved

Neal Ford published a book titled *The Productive Programmer* (O'Reilly), and I've always liked the scenario he put forward involving the deployment of one's application. It takes only three steps: run the proper scripts in the database, copy the DLLs to the correct server(s), and update the config files for database connections, routing, permissions, and so on.

It is simple and straightforward, and takes 15–20 minutes. You'll do this only once, maybe twice, a week.

Ford then adds a "what if?"—what if the project lasts eight months? That's:

- Doing 64 deployments (even more at the end of an iteration and the final push)
- 64 * 15 minutes = 960 minutes = 16 hours = 2 workdays

This is an optimistic two days. Inevitably we forget a step, or one changes slightly, and then we're spending a chunk of time tracking it down to fix it, which costs even more time.

Ford goes on to point out that if it takes less than two days to automate the process, we're good to go. But what if it takes three days to automate it? Is it worth it? I would argue yes. Automating is similar to test-driven development: there is an up-front cost for research and infrastructure. Once that infrastructure is in place, augmenting and improving the automation is modest. Of course, you need to keep your eye on how deep the rabbit hole is so as not to polish endlessly.

Saving Time with Automation

Several of the people I have encountered using PowerShell write scripts for many of their daily tasks. They do this because they know they'll probably do the task more than once, and when they do, the script will save time. Plus, PowerShell is great for doing ad hoc work and refactoring it for more formal solutions.

Here's an example of taking ad hoc PowerShell and making it more formal:

```
function Write-Date ($Date) {$Date}
Write-Date "2/29/2010"
```

This prints the date, but 2010 wasn't a leap year. If I were the only one using Write-Date, I probably wouldn't care much. On the other hand, if I sent this to other developers/scripters, I'd be concerned about them stalling and no longer using my script if this happened, so I'd make it more formal by *typing* the $Date parameter.

```
function Write-Date ([datetime]$Date) {$Date}
```

Now this will throw an error:

```
Write-Date "2/29/2010"

Write-Date : Cannot process argument transformation on parameter 'Date'. Cannot
convert value "2/29/2010" to type "System.DateTime". Error: "String was not
recognized as a valid DateTime."
```

Scripting the solution creates living documentation of what and how things were done. The script can be checked into a version control system and can be rolled back when problems hit. Down the road, these scripts can be blended into larger, more scalable solutions for working with many machines, DLLs, and configuration files.

As a final note and again echoing Neal Ford, "Finding innovative solutions to problems makes it easier to solve similar problems in the future." This rings true when applying PowerShell to so many aspects of daily development work. Plus, the more you use PowerShell, the faster you learn how to wield it. When that happens, that three-day task becomes two days, then one day, and soon you have a library of composable PowerShell functions whose whipuptitude factor lets you knock out automation in no time.

So, to get our creative, innovative juices flowing, let's take a look at some of the possibilities and some of the scripts that top PowerShell MVPs use on a regular basis.

Adding Aliases to Your PowerShell Profile

Many developers use different editors to get their jobs done. Rather than navigating through mouse clicks to get to a shortcut, you can put the following two aliases in your PowerShell $Profile. After setting this up, you can also pass filenames to the aliases, and that file will open in the editor.

```
set-alias npp "${env:ProgramFiles(x86)}\Notepad++\notepad++.exe"
set-alias tp  "${env:ProgramFiles(x86)}\TextPad 5\TextPad.exe"
```

Creating an alias to point at an executable is only one option; you can also create an alias for the functions you define or for the ones that ship with PowerShell.

Adding Variables and Functions to Your PowerShell Profile

As you gain experience with PowerShell and work on different tasks, you'll find yourself wanting to automate more and more. Take a look at the following shortcuts.

The ql Function

The following function is ql, which stands for *quote list*.

```
function ql {$args} # quote list
```

This is a Perl-ism. It was first seen in the wild when used by Bruce Payette, cofounder of PowerShell. Let's see what you can do with it.

If I want to create a list of letters, both of these produce an array. The ql version saves 12 characters.

```
$letters = "a", "b", "c", "d"
$letters = ql a b c d
```

This is very useful when you want to get something done in a one-liner on the command line. When powering through solutions quickly either at the command line or in your scripts, typing fewer characters and lines of code results in fewer errors and faster answers.

Adding Variables to $Profile

The PowerShell $Profile is run automatically when a session is started, and it's a great place to stash variables containing information you usually are looking for and forget, like the name of your email server.

```
$PSEmailServer = "mail.test.com"
```

This variable can then be used like so:

```
Send-MailMessage -SmtpServer $PSEmailServer `
    -From test@xyz.com `
    -To test@xyz.com `
    -Body "This is a test"
```

Storing variables in the PowerShell $Profile is only the beginning. You can create functions and aliases and import PowerShell modules too. A couple words of caution, though: if you move to a new machine or rebuild your box, you'll need to rebuild your profile. Also, if helping a coworker out, you won't have your favorite customizations available.

 After editing your $Profile, you can make the changes available in your current PowerShell session by running it again by dot-sourcing it like this:

```
PS C:\> . $Profile
```

Adding Custom PowerShell Functions

Often, when I'm working with different Visual Studio projects and want to quickly get to the directories from the command line, I'll try the following scripts.

Here we're setting up a function to do a change directory (cd). This makes it quick to access an area we need. Plus, we can use tab completion at the command line to cycle through the different ones we've set up.

```
function cdPowerShell { cd "c:\scripts\client\PowerShell" }
```

As an alternative, we can also create a new drive:

```
New-PSDrive -Name P -PSProvider FileSystem
    -Root C:\scripts\client\PowerShell
```

Now we can simply type P: Enter to get to where we need to go.

Quick Access to Launching Visual Studio Solutions

I work on several Visual Studio projects for clients. I always have a PowerShell prompt and ISE open. For each *.sln* I work on, I set up a PowerShell function as follows:

```
function vsTest { & "C:\temp\Test.sln" }
```

This lets me type vs and then Tab to cycle through all the functions I have available. When I find the one I like, I press Enter, the Visual Studio IDE launches with the correct solution, and I'm in business. This is a great way to save time and effort.

When you're working on projects, these simple techniques will let you power through finding and launching tools that you need, cutting down on the navigation, point-and-click routine.

Learning these tidbits helps you get more comfortable with PowerShell, become more productive, and begin to augment your workflow to make your life simpler when working on Windows machines.

Remote Desktop Connection

A *remote desktop connection* lets you sit at a computer and connect to a remote computer in a different location. I always need to remote to another box, and I'm always forgetting machine names or more are added to solve load problems.

 I prefer the keyboard over the mouse.

Figure A-1. Remote desktop machine names

I prefer direct access over navigating icons and menus; it's faster. In the following script, we *type* the parameters as a `Switch`. From there, we check for their existence in the `if` statements.

I like this approach for a couple of reasons. A handful of scripts can get a lot done. We capture the names of the boxes we want to connect to so we don't need to memorize them. Then, we can leverage Tab completion in the console to get the information we want quickly (see Figure A-1).

```
function rdp {
    param (
        [Switch]$ClientSQLBox,
        [Switch]$ClientDev,
        [Switch]$ClientIntegrationBox,
        [Switch]$ClientQABox
    )

    if($ClientSQLBox)          { $server = 'ClientSQLBox' }
    if($ClientDev)             { $server = 'ClientDev' }
    if($ClientIntegrationBox)  { $server = 'ClientIntegrationBox' }
    if($ClientQABox)           { $server = 'ClientQABox' }

    if($server) { mstsc /v:$server }
}
```

In the PowerShell v3 ISE, we type **rdp**, then hyphen (-), which tells IntelliSense to get a remote desktop connection. As you can see, we can easily pick the machine we want to connect to on that screen.

 Truth be told, I prefer PowerShell remoting. If PowerShell is installed on your machine and the target box, you can run `Enable-PSRemoting` on both.

Test to see if you can reach the target machine like this:

```
Invoke-Command -ComputerName M1 -ScriptBlock {hostname}
```

Here is the pithy way:

```
icm M1 {hostname}
```

This should return `M1` from the remote machine or an error describing why it could not connect.

Furthermore, if we're in the PowerShell console, we can type rdp, then hyphen, and then keep pressing the Tab key to cycle through each of the boxes. Upon finding the one that we want, we simply press Enter, and we're off connecting to that box.

The rdp script is simple to create and lets me automate a task that I'll do a few times a week. There are numerous other tasks I repeat over and over. Let's see how to automate some of them.

Starting Another PowerShell Session

Often, when working at the command line or in ISE, you'll want to fire up another PowerShell session for testing or running an operation that takes a while and slows progress. Out of the box, you can use Start-Process, which is aliased to Start.

```
PS C:\> Start PowerShell
```

We can wrap this in a function, Start-PowerShell. You can choose to alias this to whatever you'd like—for example, sps.

```
function Start-PowerShell {
    Start PowerShell
}
```

This ad hoc function can now be improved on. There are many times I want to test something in another PowerShell session and be sure that it works without my profile. Here goes:

```
function Start-PowerShell {
    param (
        [Switch]$NoProfile
    )

    if($NoProfile) {
        Start PowerShell -Args -NoProfile
    } else {
        Start PowerShell
    }
}
```

Now I can type Start-<Tab> -no, which will launch another PowerShell console window without loading my profile—a big timesaver.

Start-Process is versatile; following are some more things you can do with it.

Start-Process Can Do More

The Start-Process cmdlet can also launch a web page in your default browser. From the command line, we can fire up searches on Google, for example.

```
function Search-Google {
    param(
        [Parameter(ValueFromPipeline=$true)]
```

```
        [string]$query
    )

    Process {
        Start "https://www.google.com/search?q=$query"
    }
}
```

Here we launch three tabs in our default browser—one each for `win32_service`, `win_bios`, and `powershell`.

```
ql win32_service win_bios powershell | Search-Google
```

Using `Start` to launch a browser and search Google is great, but let's use this cmdlet to do something more practical. Typically when I'm working on a project, I need to have several web pages open—one each for the continuous integration server, the bug tracking system, the agile management tool, and a timesheet tracking tool, just to name a few.

```
function Show-CI        { Start "http://CIServer   }
function Show-Bugs      { Start "http://BugServer  }
function Show-Agile     { Start "http://AgileServer }
function Show-Timesheet { Start "http://TimeSheet   }
```

Now I can launch each web page from the command line, eliminating the use of the mouse to navigate to the page—time saved!

Finally, when I come in on Monday, after my machine is rebooted, I have a function, `Show-WorkTool`, that will fire up all those web pages in a single shot:

```
function Show-WorkTool {
    Show-CI
    Show-Bugs
    Show-Agile
    Show-Timesheet
}
```

Using PowerShell's Tokenizer

As you create larger and larger PowerShell scripts, developing the habit of organizing functions into separate files and loading modules is important for two reasons: managing complexity and maintaining the ability to reason through what you've built.

By developing this habit, you can look at a directory listing and see at a glance what makes up the system you're building. Plus, if you're working on these scripts with others, you'll significantly reduce conflicts while checking in when developing at this granular level.

However, there may be times when you are working with other people's scripts, and they may have chosen to keep all of the functions in a single script file or module.

A Get-Function script will help. Walk up to any directory that contains scripts or modules, type **Get-Function**, and press Enter.

This script will:

- Read each file
- Tokenize
- Extract the function name
- Extract the line number the function is on

Tokenizing is the process of breaking up a stream of text into words, phrases, symbols, or other meaningful elements called *tokens*. The list of tokens becomes input for further processing, such as finding a function name.

```
Function Get-Function ([string]$Pattern, [string]$Path="$pwd") {

    $parser = [System.Management.Automation.PSParser]

    $(ForEach( $file in Get-ChildItem $Path `
                -Recurse -Include *.ps1, *.psm1) {

        $content = [IO.File]::ReadAllText($file.FullName)
        $tokens  = $parser::Tokenize($content, [ref] $null)
        $count   = $tokens.Count

        for($idx=0; $idx -lt $count; $idx += 1) {
            if($tokens[$idx].Content -eq 'function') {

                $targetToken = $tokens[$idx+1]

                New-Object PSObject -Property @{
                    FileName     = $file.FullName
                    FunctionName = $targetToken.Content
                    Line         = $targetToken.StartLine
                } | Select FunctionName, FileName, Line
            }
        }
    }) | Where {$_.FunctionName -match $Pattern}
}
```

As an example, we'll get all the functions defined in the PSDiagnostics module delivered with PowerShell. Remember, you can also pipe the results to Out-GridView, as shown in Figure A-2.

The result shows the name of the function found and where it is in the file that contains it:

```
PS C:> Get-Function $PSHOME\Modules\PSDiagnostics

FunctionName            Line FileName
------------            ---- --------
Start-Trace               22 PSDiagnostics.psm1
Stop-Trace                98 PSDiagnostics.psm1
```

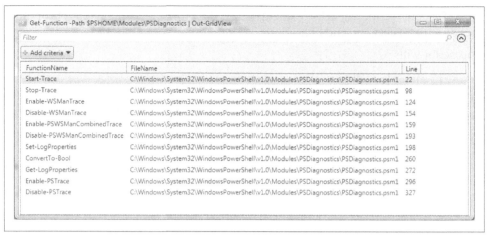

Figure A-2. Get-Function piped to Out-GridView

```
Enable-WSManTrace              124 PSDiagnostics.psm1
Disable-WSManTrace             154 PSDiagnostics.psm1
Enable-PSWSManCombinedTrace    159 PSDiagnostics.psm1
Disable-PSWSManCombinedTrace   193 PSDiagnostics.psm1
Set-LogProperties              198 PSDiagnostics.psm1
ConvertTo-Bool                 260 PSDiagnostics.psm1
Get-LogProperties              272 PSDiagnostics.psm1
Enable-PSTrace                 296 PSDiagnostics.psm1
Disable-PSTrace                327 PSDiagnostics.psm1
```

This script, `Get-Function`, helps you find your way around scripts and modules, both your own and those of others. This becomes very important as the number of scripts and modules you are working with increases.

Next we'll look at how we can work with tools that have existed for years and how PowerShell can automate solutions that will help us become more productive.

PowerShell and Older Tools

PowerShell lets you get creative. It takes a little time and investment to learn how things fit together, but it is totally worth it. For example, tools you have been working with for a long time probably output text or XML that can be easily consumed by PowerShell. This can be a great area to add some PowerShell automation and spin up productive solutions. Let's take a look at some examples.

Subversion

Subversion (SVN) sports a command-line utility that lets you interact with svn repositories. Using this utility in our PowerShell directory, we get these results:

```
PS C:\PoSh> svn info

Path: .
Working Copy Root Path: C:\PoSH
URL: https://wush.net/svn/finked/PoSH/trunk
Repository Root: https://wush.net/svn/finked
Repository UUID: 10d2a5bc-2623-0410-be31-c5168cbc2b14
Revision: 1574
Node Kind: directory
Schedule: normal
Last Changed Author: finked
Last Changed Rev: 1574
Last Changed Date: 2012-02-09 20:37:32 -0500 (Thu, 09 Feb 2012)
```

After a little digging, you'll discover that Subversion lets you retrieve these results in an XML format, by specifying the --xml option.

```
PS C:\PoSh> svn info --xml
```

Now, here is where we get creative. We know that we can use the XML accelerator [xml] in PowerShell and then use dot notation to pull out details.

```
PS C:\PoSh> ([xml](svn --xml info)).info.entry

kind       : dir
path       : .
revision   : 1574
url        : https://wush.net/svn/finked/PoSH/trunk
repository : repository
wc-info    : wc-info
commit     : commit
```

We're now programmatically accessing individual details from text returned by a Subversion command. No parsing, no praying!

Displaying SVN info on your PowerShell prompt

How can we make this even more useful? Using the previous technique, say we want to see how many files are not under version control, how many items are scheduled for addition, and how many items have been modified. Plus, we don't want to type anything in. We simply want to do a cd and see this information at a glance (see Figure A-3).

The script. Add the following script to your PowerShell $Profile, and you'll get a new prompt. By writing a function named prompt, you are now substituting the built-in one for yours.

 You need to have the Subversion command-line utility installed for this Subversion script to work.

There are several goodies in this script—overriding the built-in prompt, working with the $host variable, and using the switch statement.

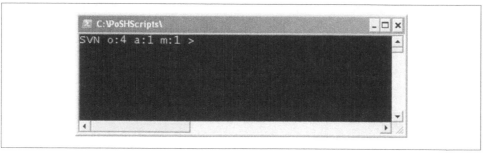

Figure A-3. SVN PowerShell prompt

> The switch statement is the most powerful statement in the PowerShell language. It combines pattern matching, branching, and iteration all into a single control structure.

Issuing the svn st command returns a list of files. The switch statement will iterate over them line by line, and the -regex parameter lets us specify a regular expression in the branching. Each iteration will tally the accumulators $other, $added, and $modified, which are ultimately displayed as the prompt shown in Figure A-3.

```
function prompt {
    $host.ui.rawui.WindowTitle = $(Get-Location)

    if(Test-Path .svn) {
        switch -regex (svn st) {
            "^\?" {$other+=1}
            "^A" {$added+=1}
            "^M" {$modified+=1}
            default {}
        }

        $prompt_string = "SVN o:$other a:$added m:$modified >"
    } else {
        $prompt_string = "PS >"
    }

    Write-Host ($prompt_string) -NoNewline -ForegroundColor yellow

    return " "
}
```

> Google "powershell prompt" and you'll get hits on how creative people have gotten with this. Here are two examples that take the Subversion approach, connecting the PowerShell prompt to a version control system:
>
> - "A Mercurial PowerShell Prompt" (*http://bit.ly/c1OGJa*)
> - "Better Git with PowerShell" (*http://bit.ly/vmQ1y3*)

Faster, Faster—The Light Is Turning Red

As in any language, in PowerShell there are ways to shuffle the code to get more performance. For example, I found a great performance boost when I was porting some spell-correction Python code posted by Peter Norvig, director of research at Google (*http://bit.ly/I7YEJ3*).

This technique uses a training text file that contains about 5,500 lines and 100,000 words. The PowerShell script reads the file, splitting up the lines, capturing the individual words, and creating a container of unique words.

I'll show you the first approach I came up with, SlowTrain, and then the faster improved version, FastTrain. It's good to see this in action so you can keep in mind that there are alternate ways to structure your PowerShell scripts and get significant performance increases.

SlowTrain

Let's train a probability model, which is a fancy way of saying, "count how many times each word occurs, using the function train." We'll extract the words and create an index of unique words. We'll use .NET regular expressions, and then add each word as a key to a hash table. The result will be a container of unique words.

```
function SlowTrain($text) {

    $h = @{}
    [regex]::split($text.ToLower(), '\W+') |
        ForEach {
            $h[$_] =''
        }
    $h
}
```

Here we'll read the file, and then pass it to the trainer.

```
# Read the file
$Text = [IO.File]::ReadAllText( "$pwd\holmes.txt" )

# Create the unique words
SlowTrain $Text
```

Calling SlowTrain will take a little more than three seconds to return. Next up, we'll rework this SlowTrain into FastTrain and go from a three-second response time to subsecond.

FastTrain

With FastTrain, you will see that the following code produces a subsecond response time:

```
function FastTrain($text) {

    $h = @{}
    ForEach ($word in [regex]::split($text.ToLower(), '\W+') )
    {
        $h[$word] = ''
    }
    $h
}
```

We reworked the code by using the ForEach statement, resulting in processing that's six times faster.

ForEach-Object Versus ForEach Statement

There is the reason SlowTrain is slow: it uses the ForEach-Object. We piped the results of the [regex] to it, and that is a bottleneck for this type of application. Switching to the ForEach statement solves the problem. For more information, check out my blog post "PowerShell—Four For Loops and their timings," at *http://bit.ly/nTNMG6*.

Summary

PowerShell is an interpreted, dynamic language, and there are performance considerations to think about when applying it. The great news is that, because it is built on .NET, there are far fewer roadblocks to delivering a broad range of solutions to multiple users.

 PowerShell optimizes the person, not the CPU.

I hope this spectrum of examples illustrates PowerShell's reach. This list is very short, so I encourage you to use your preferred search engine to seek out how broad and deep the PowerShell community is and what it is sharing.

Whether you're connecting remotely, building spell checkers, or launching browsers or other applications, remember: *if you repeat it, PowerShell it.*

Running PowerShell with the .NET 4.0 Runtime

Here are the steps for configuring PowerShell v2 to run with the .NET 4.0 runtime. (This StackOverflow link has more information: *http://bit.ly/GB6gEe*.)

```
PS C:\> cd $PSHOME
PS C:\Windows\System32\WindowsPowerShell\v1.0>
    notepad .\powershell.exe.config
```

Add this XML and save the file:

```
<?xml version="1.0"?>
<configuration>
    <startup useLegacyV2RuntimeActivationPolicy="true">
        <supportedRuntime version="v4.0.30319"/>
        <supportedRuntime version="v2.0.50727"/>
    </startup>
</configuration>
```

Restart the PowerShell console, and then type **$PSVersionTable**. You should see the following entry:

```
Name                    Value
----                    -----
CLRVersion              4.0.30319.239
```

About the Author

Doug Finke, a Microsoft Most Valuable Professional (MVP) for PowerShell, is a software developer at Lab49, a company that builds advanced applications for the financial service industry. For the last 20 years, Doug has been a developer and author working with numerous technologies. You can catch up with Doug at his blog Development in a Blink at *http://dougfinke.com/blog/*.

Get even more for your money.

Join the O'Reilly Community, and register the O'Reilly books you own. It's free, and you'll get:

- $4.99 ebook upgrade offer
- 40% upgrade offer on O'Reilly print books
- Membership discounts on books and events
- Free lifetime updates to ebooks and videos
- Multiple ebook formats, DRM FREE
- Participation in the O'Reilly community
- Newsletters
- Account management
- 100% Satisfaction Guarantee

Signing up is easy:

1. **Go to: oreilly.com/go/register**
2. **Create an O'Reilly login.**
3. **Provide your address.**
4. **Register your books.**

Note: English-language books only

To order books online:
oreilly.com/store

For questions about products or an order:
orders@oreilly.com

To sign up to get topic-specific email announcements and/or news about upcoming books, conferences, special offers, and new technologies:
elists@oreilly.com

For technical questions about book content:
booktech@oreilly.com

To submit new book proposals to our editors:
proposals@oreilly.com

O'Reilly books are available in multiple DRM-free ebook formats. For more information:
oreilly.com/ebooks

Spreading the knowledge of innovators   oreilly.com

Have it your way.